A PLACE LIKE MISSISSIPPI

A PLACE LIKE MISSISSIPPI

A JOURNEY THROUGH A REAL AND
IMAGINED LITERARY LANDSCAPE

W. RALPH EUBANKS

TIMBER PRESS
PORTLAND, OREGON

*For Colleen, who makes possible all things in
my life that seem impossible,*

*and for my parents, two great Alabamians
who made me a Mississippian.*

Published in 2021 by Timber Press, Inc.

The Haseltine Building
133 S.W. Second Avenue, Suite 450
Portland, Oregon 97204-3527
timberpress.com

Printed in China

Text design by Hillary Caudle
Jacket design by Kimberly Glyder and Hillary Caudle

ISBN 978-1-60469-958-6

Catalog records for this book are available from the
Library of Congress and the British Library.

You can get there from here, though
there's no going home.

Everywhere you go will be somewhere
you've never been. Try this:

head south on Mississippi 49, one-
by-one mile markers ticking off

another minute of your life. Follow this
to its natural conclusion—dead end

at the coast, the pier at Gulfport where
riggings of shrimp boats are loose stitches

in a sky threatening rain.

—Natasha Trethewey, "Theories of Time and Space" from *Native Guard*

CONTENTS

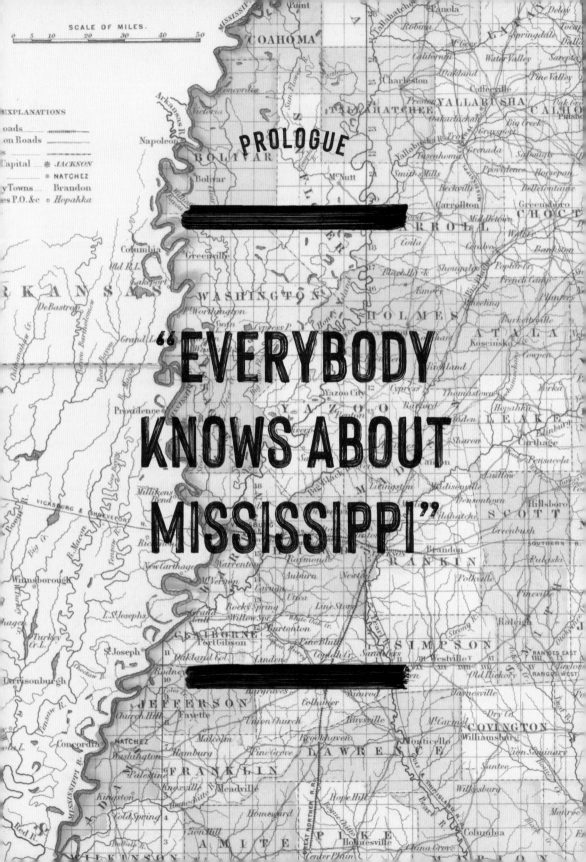

PROLOGUE

"EVERYBODY KNOWS ABOUT MISSISSIPPI"

Mississippi . . . is a place where great literature somehow blossomed in a field of vast illiteracy.

—Curtis Wilkie, *Assassins, Eccentrics, Politicians, and Other Persons of Interest*

T O A FIRST-TIME VISITOR, Mississippi's rural landscape brings to mind solitude and loneliness, a place from which one escapes rather than returns. Yet once the bright and pure quiet of a Mississippi country setting consumes your senses, you begin to feel as if you are in a place comfortably frozen in time. Off the beaten path of four-lane highways, on two-lane blacktops that wind through the rolling hills of the Piney Woods or run the vast stretches of flat Delta land, the hush of the setting is punctuated by tin-roofed barns and houses both large and small. Even close to a small town or suburban development, the land feels remote and holds the power to transfix your gaze. If you slow down and look closely—or even stop to walk around and seek out local inhabitants—you'll understand why some of the loneliest spaces and most decrepit buildings in the state inspire writers to move them from the landscape to the page. This migration of Mississippi from the real to the imagined is a source of pride for its residents. Whether it is a tree-lined street in the Belhaven neighborhood of Jackson or a narrow stretch of the Chunky River that weaves through the hills outside of Meridian, many writers have taken a piece of the state's landscape and populated it with a world that mirrors and magnifies the space that inspired it.

Eudora Welty recognized Mississippi as a place that held mystery. In *The Golden Apples*, she sought to expand upon the land's seemingly unknowable qualities through the fictional setting of Morgana. The result

9

is a town in the Yazoo-Mississippi Delta as complex as the landscape itself. Welty combines the red clay with the hayfield and the cotton field, and throws in the Old Natchez Trace for good measure. Morgana could be any small town in the state.

But it was not the Delta that inspired her story "June Recital," which is set in Morgana. Instead, it was the very street she lived on in Jackson, Pinehurst Street, across from the Belhaven University Music Department where she would hear the constant practicing of piano. In the afterword to her Morgana stories Welty writes, "I began to hear, in what kept coming across the street . . . the recurring dreams of youth, inescapable, never to be renounced, naming themselves over and over again." Those "recurring dreams of youth" were poured into her character Virgie Rainey and transported to her imaginary Morgana.

Welty is not alone in creating a confluence of place and memory on the page. Often there is a melding of settings by Mississippi writers rather than the pure re-creation of a solitary location. When Brad Watson set parts of his novel *The Heaven of Mercury* along the banks of the Chunky River, a popular spot for canoeists and fishermen, he mixed together family stories and childhood memories as well as accounts of the riverbank as it exists today. "I have it in my mind that in my parents' and grandparents' days, excursions to the Chunky River were even more common than they were in my time. There were a

A Mississippi Delta cotton field.

lot fewer ways for young people to entertain themselves in those times," Watson recalls. But it was also a memory from his childhood that led him to use the river as a setting. "Young people have gone there for a long time to have fun in the summer, so a picnic there makes sense. During my family's leanest times my brothers and I asked my father one spring if we

Stuckey's Bridge over the Chunky River, just outside Meridian.

would get to have a vacation at the beach that year. My father laughed and said, 'We can't even afford a vacation to *Chunky* this year.'"

When a place is experienced through the lens of the real and the imagined, whether through our own eyes or those of a writer, it takes on a heightened sense of reality. When Nina Simone sings "Everybody knows about Mississippi, goddam," images of the violent, turbulent civil rights era come to mind and those scenes from the past become vividly real. Natasha Trethewey evokes a different image in "Theories of Time and Space" when she implores you, her reader, to head south on U.S. Route 49 until it dead-ends in the coastal town of Gulfport, asks you to walk on its artificial beach, and then reminds you to "Bring only what you must carry—tome of memory, its random blank pages." These two impressions of Mississippi—one forged in anger and the other in a mixture of love, memory, loss, and recovery—have much in common. What each writer reveals are the complex emotions that a place so beautiful yet so confounding can bring about.

Whether the pages of your notebook are blank or filled with memory, Mississippi's landscape is one that feeds the work of its writers. When I returned to Mississippi in 1999 to begin research for what I thought would be

13

a narrative history of the Mississippi State Sovereignty Commission—a civil rights–era, pro-segregation spy agency run and funded by the state for nearly twenty years—I found myself drawn in by the land itself because it was this landscape that made me a writer. That narrative history became a memoir and place became central to the story I decided to tell. What I realized upon returning was how much of my imagination was threaded together in Mississippi, so much so that it affected the way I looked at the entire world. Growing up on a farm, I also knew the rhythm of the land, with pictures imprinted on my mind of what it looked like in each of the four seasons. That is why my hometown and my farm are characters as much as the people I interviewed and wrote about in *Ever Is a Long Time*.

This transformation of Mississippi's landscape into the canon of American letters is one that makes many ask, "Why does this land"—a very poor rural state with a high rate of illiteracy—"inspire and produce so many writers?" While many have sought to find the answer to this great anomaly, some, like Mississippi-born literary critic Noel Polk, facetiously ascribe it to the air Mississippians breathe and the water they drink. In his book *Tell About the South*, Fred Hobson notes that, "The Southerner, more than any other Americans, has felt he had something to explain, to justify, to defend, or to affirm." John Grisham believes Mississippi's outsized literary output has its origins in suffering, but a particular type of suffering. "Suffering that has been self-inflicted by slavery, war, poverty, injustice, intolerance. Great conflict produces great art, and Mississippi has its share of both." Poet Natasha Trethewey also notes that the pain in Mississippi, like the pain in other parts of the world, leads to art. She writes, "In his memorial to William Butler Yeats, W. H. Auden wrote 'Mad Ireland hurt you into poetry.' Likewise, my native land, my South, my Mississippi . . . hurt me into poetry, inflicting my first wound."

Like Ireland, Mississippi's history is filled with suffering that must be explained; it is a place that comes alive in its stories and inspires those stories, which flow through every bend of its winding rivers and across every piece of land within its borders. It is the beauty of the land mixed with the state's complex history that inspires and perplexes its writers. That is the burden one feels when writing about Mississippi, because it is a place that everyone knows about—or at least claims to—yet few are willing to understand.

For better or for worse, Mississippi has become a metaphor for the entire South and for that matter even the entire nation. As Malcolm X said, "As far as I am concerned, Mississippi is anywhere south of the Canadian border." A story about race set in Mississippi is as much about the sins of the nation as it is about the sins of the Magnolia State. The American South, and Mississippi in particular, have "existed never so much as a literal place than as a figurative one," writes noted historian and Mississippi native Joseph Crespino.

"The Southern writer is forced from all sides to make his gaze extend beyond the surface, beyond mere problems, until it touches that realm which is the concern of prophets and poets," Flannery O'Connor wrote in her essay "Some Aspects of the Grotesque in Southern Fiction." She very well could have been writing about Mississippi writers, since they all feel the need to describe the place with the greatest of intimacy yet in a way that makes what is unique about Mississippi resonate with an air of universality. It is Mississippians' obsession with place, people, politics, and history that leads its writers to use the state to contemplate larger existential arguments with the greater world. The extremes in Mississippi's politics, history, and people leads to what Brad Watson calls "a high octane" treatment of place, which in turn leads to more critical poking and pondering. Perhaps that is why one of the most quoted lines from William Faulkner's *Absalom, Absalom!* comes from his character Quentin Compson, who, when asked to explain the South says, "You can't understand it. You would have to be born there." When pressed about why he hates the South: "'I dont hate it,'

15

"EVERYBODY KNOWS ABOUT MISSISSIPPI"

Sunset over an antebellum house in Benoit.

Quentin said, quickly, at once, immediately; 'I dont hate it,' he said. *I dont hate it* he thought, panting in the cold air, the iron New England dark: *I dont. I dont! I dont hate it! I dont hate it!*"

It is hard to imagine a character in the western novels of Wallace Stegner, in Sherwood Anderson's Winesburg, Ohio, or Edith Wharton's New York pondering how much they love or hate the place they are from as Quentin Compson does. The West, Northeast, and Midwest each have

their own unique history, yet its residents are not asked to explain their affection and devotion to a place—as well as the history of that place—the way those of the Magnolia State are asked to explain a place with a legacy of lost battles, whether those happened during the Civil War, the civil rights movement, or today. That is why Mississippi has become the South writ large—and even the nation writ large—because it is a place that inspires its residents to contemplate how much they love it as well as how much they hate it more than any other state in the Union.

Within the work of every Mississippi writer exists a tension between the history of the characters and actual historic events, between the history of place and the region's idea of itself. Historical events are seen as metaphor, while a character's history is viewed as the real thing. Faulkner's *Absalom, Absalom!* is a novel about history, and it is the South's history of slavery and miscegenation—and the shame sometimes associated with that history—that propels the narrative. The main character, Thomas Sutpen, is framed in the narrative as a man with "no past," but he is actually a man with a hidden past, which Faulkner slowly unspools, revealing how the past is a living force, one that frames and shapes our sense of the present.

Thomas Sutpen in some ways is a metaphor for Mississippi, which is a place that sometimes avoids its past rather than confronting it. Perhaps that is why every Mississippi writer feels in some way that the past can never be escaped. It is largely this inability to shut the door on the past that fuels the work of Mississippi's writers, who feel the need to explain these shards of history. It certainly has provided the backdrop for my work as a writer and essayist who focuses on the American South. I sense a profound need to serve as a clarifying force in understanding Mississippi and the South. To find a good Mississippi story, I always say, "explore the silences," for it is within the parts of our history we have chosen to shroud in silence in which our best stories reside. My writing life involves the pursuit of those silences.

But the idea of Mississippi's landscape and history serving as the inspiration for its writers is not merely an outgrowth of the aftermath of the Civil War or a twentieth-century literary movement, or a movement that has its origins in the work of William Faulkner. Mississippi's indigenous people are the earliest creators of literature in the state, with an oral tradition that also focused on explaining the past, a past that in some ways has been lost. Yet their literary voices remain in the names of places that dot the landscape: Biloxi, Tunica, Pascagoula, Yazoo, Tishomingo, Yalobusha, Tallahatchie, Itta Bena, Yockanookany, and, from my native Piney Woods, Okatoma. It is in the names of

Panther Swamp National Wildlife Refuge, outside Yazoo City.

these places that this state's native people contributed to Mississippi literature's distinctive voice, described by writer Willie Morris as "the mysterious, lost euphonious litany."

A journey through the terrain that inspires Mississippi writers is one taken through both real and imagined places, where sometimes what is imagined seems real and what is real seems imaginary. The centrality of place to Mississippi writers is what makes the real and imagined so closely intertwined, whether it is Faulkner's Jefferson and the university town of Oxford, Elizabeth Spencer's town of Lacey from *The Voice at the Back Door* and Carrollton, or Steve Yarbrough's imagined Delta town of Loring and his hometown of Indianola. While those beautiful and mysterious Native American names dapple the landscape, keeping a lost piece of the state's past alive, Mississippi as a place is changing and evolving, even in places like the Delta, where much seems to be frozen in time and the past only seems to melt along the edges. Still, change can be difficult to embrace.

Change, particularly cultural change, may be difficult to accept in Mississippi because it is a place held rapt by its own mythology as well as cultural rituals that sustain those myths. Yet the patchwork of eighty-two counties that make up Mississippi are indeed changing, and those changes reverberate from the piers along the Mississippi Sound in the Gulf of Mexico right up to the Tennessee state line at Memphis. Sometimes that change feels like a ruin that cannot be rebuilt, its original structure now compromised by constant battering. It is the rebuilding from the ruins that drives the work of the state's writers and allows their work to be so central not only to the culture of Mississippi but also to American literature. As Jackson-based writer Katy Simpson Smith has noted, to be a Mississippi writer today is not to write about a state "dripping with Spanish moss and punctuated by mockingbird song," but instead to explore "surprising intersections, where violence within the self had become as important as violence across racial lines, where poverty was nuanced rather than made perverse, where families were built from intentional love rather than tied to tortured bloodlines."

"To understand the world, you must first understand a place like Mississippi" are words that are said to have come from William Faulkner, but were more likely to have been attributed to Faulkner by his fellow Mississippian Willie Morris. The story I've heard is that either Willie thought Faulkner had said it, or maybe he *wanted* Faulkner to have said it. Whatever the origin of these words, they are true and that is why they have become the mantra of every writer who works within the borders of this state. If you can find where the past and the present intersect within Mississippi, you can indeed understand the world. The idea that Mississippi is a place larger than life serves as inspiration to writers who were born there but work elsewhere. These writers have never been able to shake their conscience free of the place because in Mississippi nothing is ever escaped. This sense also inspires those Mississippi writers who now claim this state as home and seek to understand its wounds and imperfections as they create poems and stories that spring from this soil. In the pages that follow, both the words of these writers and images of the places that inspired them will reveal how a little state that rests alongside the banks of a great and mighty river has made so many significant contributions to American letters, carrying an outsized role in the national imagination. The answer lies in a landscape that pairs ordinariness with beauty, magic with madness, and mystery with magnificence.

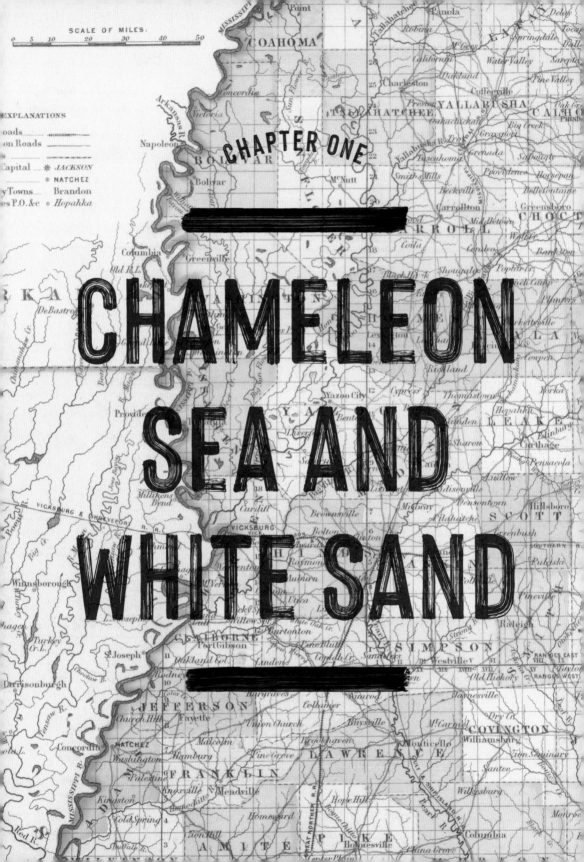

CHAPTER ONE

CHAMELEON SEA AND WHITE SAND

where that old flag still hangs, I return
      to Mississippi, state that made a crime

of me—mulatto, half-breed—native
      in my native land, this place they'll bury me.

—Natasha Trethewey, "South"

The Biloxi Lighthouse, erected in 1848, has become a
symbol of the resilience of the Mississippi Gulf Coast.

*T*HE MISSISSIPPI GULF COAST EXISTS apart from the rest of the
state not just because of its bays, bayous, and beaches. What makes
the Gulf Coast different is its intermingled, polyglot culture and communities. It is not unusual to have the words of the original native people dot
the landscape of this state, and on the Gulf Coast, the rivers that contribute to the area's unique geography are named for three major native tribes
that once dominated the region: Biloxi, Pascagoula, and Tchoutacabouffa.
Together these native names and the ghosts they evoke exist alongside
the remnants of French, Creole, Spanish, and African cultures that all
intermingled here. Mississippi's twenty-six miles of white sandy beaches
along the Gulf of Mexico form the largest and longest artificial beach in the
United States. While the beach is scenic, it is also practical: it was fortified
by the U.S. Army Corps of Engineers, beginning in the early 1950s, to stem
seawall erosion. Despite a historic marker nearby, few realize the glistening stretch of beach in the town of Biloxi was the scene of what the *New
York Times* called "the worst race riot in Mississippi history."

Despite receiving federal funding, in 1960 the Gulf Coast beaches
were unlawfully segregated, and black beachgoers were relegated to small
and less well-maintained parts of this long stretch of sand. Local physician
Gilbert Mason led a series of what he called wade-ins at the beach. "Local
practice reserved God's sunrises and sunsets over the glistening waters
and white sands of Biloxi beach for the exclusive enjoyment of white

CHAMELEON SEA AND WHITE SAND

ABOVE The Biloxi beach "wade-ins" in 1960, led by Gilbert Mason.
BELOW A view of the Mississippi Sound from the beach at Gulfport.

folks," Mason wrote in his memoir, *Beaches, Blood, and Ballots*. "For a man who loved swimming and who had gloried in the free use of the parks in Chicago and Washington, D.C., the idea that a marvelous oak-lined public beach was forbidden territory was just too much to abide." At the wade-in on April 24, 1960, hundreds of peaceful black protesters were beaten by a mob of whites carrying pool cues, clubs, chains, blackjacks, lead pipes, and baseball bats. The white sand was stained with blood, and Dr. Mason had to treat many of those who were beaten. In spite of the constant threat of violence, Gilbert Mason refused to give up, hosting another wade-in protest in 1963. In Mississippi civil rights history, the wade-ins have been overshadowed by the Jackson lunch counter sit-ins and the famed Freedom Rides, but it was the wade-ins that served as a litmus test for future challenges to segregation.

Today these beaches are merely a gleaming trap for tourists. On foggy mornings the sand glimmers in the early coastal light reflecting off the Gulf. The moss-covered live oaks and tall pine trees complete the setting of a place that feels like paradise and stands apart in a state largely known for its dirt-under-the-fingernails agrarian history.

U.S. Route 49 in Mississippi runs across the expanse of the Delta, along the edge of Hill Country, directly through the Piney Woods, and ends at a pier in the coastal town of Gulfport. The coast is a place associated with the names of two powerful storms that felt like an ending: Camille and Katrina. Yet the highway's terminus at the Gulf of Mexico actually marks the beginning of Mississippi rather than the end. It is because of those life-altering storms on the Gulf Coast that we see how Mississippi can be remade, reshaped, and transformed. Reinvention is built into the social fabric of the Gulf Coast, and that is why a journey through the literary landscape of the Magnolia State must begin in this coastal region once described by Mississippi Delta writer Hodding Carter II as "a soft, near-tropic abode of chameleon sea and white sand."

Since its settlement, the landscape of the Gulf Coast has served as an inspiration for artists. George Ohr, known as the "mad potter of Biloxi," found the clay for what is known as the first art pottery in the country from the banks of Tchoutacabouffa River. He startled the art world in 1885 with six hundred pieces of pottery that he exhibited at the World's Fair in New Orleans. Painter Walter Anderson was drawn by the light of the Gulf Coast and created watercolors and drawings centered on the animals, insects, and natural beauty of the coastal landscape. He even once tied himself to a tree during a hurricane to experience the fury of nature, since the very landscape he painted was shaped by that fury. Together the visual artists and writers from Mississippi's Gulf Coast have created an alchemy of the visual and the verbal, bringing the beauty and ferocity of the landscape and its people into the written word. Like all Mississippi writers, the Gulf Coast artists seek to capture the terrifying beauty of the state in a region marked time and again by nature's devastation.

Walter Anderson's painting of Horn Island, his place of refuge.

"When we begin to imagine a future in which the places of our past no longer exist, we see *ruin*," former U.S. Poet Laureate and Mississippi Poet Laureate Natasha Trethewey writes. The ruin and destruction Trethewey references moves beyond the Gulf Coast's eroding beaches and the ancient live oak trees that were uprooted after Hurricane Katrina in 2005. That storm changed the life of Trethewey's family and many residents of the Mississippi Gulf Coast, a place Trethewey claims both as home and literary talisman.

Trethewey views her work as a poet as a means of capturing what is forgotten or not seen as a result of erasure from local and national memory. She explores how historical amnesia manifests itself on the landscape—both the physical and cultural landscape—and then shapes our view of the world. In her eyes, poetry serves as a corrective to the way we view history, the way we critique events and figures of Mississippi's and America's historical past, and the way we see the present. Trethewey's poetry inscribes her broader ideas about race, cultural identity, and the history of the South onto the psyche of her readers as well as the American literary canon. The Gulf Coast exists not simply as an external landscape that inspires her work, but it is also part of an interior landscape of the psyche that Trethewey shares with her readers.

The Gulf Coast is the setting of her first collection, *Domestic Work*, a series of poems based on the life of her maternal grandmother. Her second collection, *Bellocq's Ophelia*, uses nineteenth-century New Orleans photographer E. J. Bellocq's portraits to tell the story of a mixed-raced prostitute, who Bellocq had captured in one of his photographs. In that collection, Trethewey grapples with her own experiences of growing up in the Deep South as a light-skinned, biracial woman. In her collection, *Native Guard*, Trethewey returns to the Gulf Coast landscape and a place familiar to her from childhood: Ship Island.

Ship Island, a former fort and a place Trethewey visited regularly as a child, is a barrier island that rests eleven miles off the coast of her home-town of Gulfport. After Hurricane Camille, the forces of nature cut Ship Island in two, and the spot was called the Camille Cut. Today the wonders of engineering have rejoined what that powerful storm split asunder, cre-ating a single island of lush beach grasses, dusky scrub pines, and white sandy beaches that match those along U.S. Route 90. Today Ship Island is more like it was during Trethewey's mother's childhood than it was during Trethewey's own.

As an adult, upon arriving at Ship Island on one of the regular tour boats, one of the first things Trethewey noticed was a plaque at the fort's entry listing all the names of the Confederate soldiers who were impris-oned there. What she knew was missing was any mention of the black soldiers who were stationed there, including the members of the Second Regiment of the Louisiana Native Guards and the First Regiment of the Native Guards, which was the first officially sanctioned regi-ment of African American soldiers in the Civil War. On Ship Island, Trethewey encountered what many Americans are faced with each day: public memory, with omissions and embellishments. This missing

LEFT Ship Island Lighthouse, Gulfport.

RIGHT The Second Louisiana Native Guard on Ship Island and inspiration for Natasha Trethewey's Pulitzer Prize–winning poetry collection.

history became an interest of Trethewey's since she knew that there was a history "that I think would've been very important to have known when I was growing up and spending the Fourth of July on that island, a little black girl in Mississippi. So that's where I began. I started researching the Civil War, black soldiers, and Ship Island."

Trethewey liked the idea of both the literal and the figurative possibilities of the term "native guard." "I began to think about myself and of Mississippi history and the idea of native, I saw a way to explore the tension evident in being a native of a place that has denied full citizenship to many native sons and daughters." Trethewey's collection *Native Guard*, which won the Pulitzer Prize in Poetry in 2007, is a shining example of her belief in poetry as a "necessary utterance." For Trethewey, a poem gets its power from "its sense of justice, its ability to witness without trivializing what happened with a 'poetic' ending. It remembers without diminishing."

31

Fort Massachusetts on Ship Island, once home to the Louisiana Native Guard.

Trethewey's great theme is memory. There is the memory of her childhood on the Gulf Coast as the child of a black mother and white father whose marriage was considered illegal in Mississippi when she was born. There is the memory of the loss of her mother, murdered by her second husband when Trethewey was a young woman, an event Trethewey writes marked her as "a daughter of sorrow." It is in the memories Trethewey recalls in her poetry that we see a reflection of herself, where she wrestles with her dual consciousness of being both black and Southern as well as a child of Mississippi, a place where her very existence was deemed a crime. Yet no matter how much Trethewey wrestles with the conflicts and contradictions of her home state, it is her love of

CHAPTER ONE

Mississippi, and particularly the Gulf Coast, that shines through in her work. As she writes in "Liturgy to the Mississippi Gulf Coast":

> This is my *nostos*—my pilgrimage to the Coast, my memory,
>
>   my reckoning—
>
> native daughter: I am the Gulf Coast.

⬇

NOVELIST, MEMOIRIST, AND TWO-TIME National Book Award winner Jesmyn Ward also loves the rivers and bayous that make the Gulf Coast and her hometown of DeLisle a unique place. But more than geography, she feels connected to this land of sea and white sand because of the people she has known here, those whose spirits for her are still very much part of this landscape. "I never want to forget those who I've lost," Ward told me one spring afternoon in Pass Christian Books, her local bookstore. "And then, too, I feel as if in some respects with the type of writing that I'm trying to do, the kinds of stories that I'm trying to tell and who I am attempting to tell them about, that I'm taking on a certain responsibility. Living in Mississippi keeps me truthful and honest because I live around the people I write about."

The DeLisle Bayou lies north of the town of Pass Christian over a bridge that snakes across the Wolf River. Once you cross the bridge, you have entered the setting of Jesmyn Ward's fictional Mississippi town of Bois Sauvage. In her first novel, *Where the Line Bleeds*, the main character, Joshua, describes both Ward's fictional world as well as the real place that she loves:

> He knew that there shouldn't be anything special about Bois
> Sauvage, but there was: he knew every copse of trees, every stray

CHAMELEON SEA AND WHITE SAND

dog, every bend of every half-paved road, every uneven plane of each warped, dilapidated house, every hidden swimming hole. While the other towns of the coast shared boundaries and melted into each other so that he could only tell he was leaving one and arriving in the other by some landmark, like a Circle K or a Catholic church, Bois Sauvage dug in small on the back of the bay, isolated. Natural boundaries surrounded it on three sides. To the south, east, and west, a bayou bordered it, the same bayou that the Wolf River emptied into before it pooled into the Bay of Angels and then out to the Gulf of Mexico. There were only two roads that crossed the bayou and led out of Bois Sauvage to St. Catherine, the next town over.

Joshua was also the name of Ward's only brother, killed by a drunk driver and whose life she pays tribute to in her memoir *Men We Reaped* alongside the lives of four other young black men she knew between the ages of 19 and 31. The book serves as a memorial to these young men who died too soon and too violently. Joshua's name is not only memorialized in Ward's fiction and nonfiction work but also in a tattoo inked in a script matching his signature on the inside of Ward's right wrist. On the other wrist are the words "Love, brother."

"Just being able to see his signature on my wrist is an affirmation that he lived," she said. "'Love, brother' comes from a letter Joshua wrote me when I was in college and that is exactly how he signed it."

It is the loss of her brother and her other friends that is part of her deep connection to the Gulf Coast. Joshua's death made Ward "look at everyone else in my family and everyone else in my community and have almost a panicky feeling that makes me wonder what if I miss all of these days and then something happens to someone that I love and then I have to live with the regret of knowing that I could have had that time with that person." During her days away from the coast studying at Stanford, working in New York and then later at the University of Michigan, she felt those were places she had to be at the time but never truly felt grounded. Although Ward remains in Mississippi to heal her emotional scars, it is the beauty of her hometown of DeLisle that inspires and drives her writing.

DeLisle, fictionalized as Bois Sauvage, is the setting of Ward's two other novels, *Salvage the Bones* and *Sing, Unburied, Sing*, both National Book Award winners. (Her 2018 win for *Sing, Unburied, Sing*, made Ward the first woman to ever win two National Book Awards.) *Salvage the Bones* is a painfully poetic story of a family preparing for Hurricane Katrina and dealing with the aftermath of the storm. The post-Katrina landscape is both part of Ward's consciousness and her fiction. As she wrote in *Salvage the Bones*:

Two-time National Book Award Winner Jesmyn Ward under the live oak trees in her hometown of Delisle.

> The bayou formed by the meeting of the river and the bay is as calm as it would be on any summer day, and it is hard to tell the hurricane has been here except for where the wind dragged the water across the road and left it there. The bayou is where we had thought the water would come from, the reason we thought we were safe, but Katrina surprised everyone with her uncompromising strength, her forcefulness, the way she lingered; she made things happen that had never happened before.

A peaceful bayou along the Mississippi Gulf Coast.

Salvage the Bones is a story about community pulling together, which is part of Ward's attraction to the Gulf Coast: its strong community connections. And in spite of the changes rendered by Katrina, Ward believes DeLisle feels relatively unchanged. "DeLisle Bayou still seems very much like the same place that it was when I was a child probably because of Hurricane Katrina. The storm surge came up through Bay St. Louis and DeLisle Bayou and basically flattened everything. Perhaps that is why it still feels as wild as it did when I was growing up here."

Like *Salvage the Bones*, Ward's third novel, *Sing, Unburied, Sing*, largely takes place on the Gulf Coast. One segment of the narrative, however, is set north in the heart of Mississippi. When her husband is released from prison, the main character, Leonie, takes her children and a friend to Parchman Farm, the Mississippi State Penitentiary. It is on this trip that the reader begins to feel the characters' sense of displacement from the landscape as soon as they are more than one hundred miles from the Gulf. Told from the perspective of young Jojo, when they approach the Delta, the world seems to close in: "When we pull off the highway and onto a back road, the sky is dark blue, turning its back to us, pulling a black sheet over its shoulder." Jojo also notices that houses, so close together at home, are spread far apart here, "not like the huddle of houses in Forrest County."

Ward said that the sense of displacement her characters feel comes from her own feeling that the culture and landscape of Mississippi change "once you're north of Forrest County." For Ward, the history of the Gulf Coast, with its cultural intermingling, is what distinguishes it from the rest of Mississippi. "The French, Spanish, Indigenous, and African cultures all came together in different ways and helped shape the communities of the Gulf Coast. When you think of the Gulf Coast and its culture, it is like referring to New Orleans, in a way." It makes sense that her characters feel out of place when in the middle of the Delta, a place where Jim Crow's influence can still be felt in the people and the landscape. While the Southern myth, so strongly tied to the Delta, is part of the cultural landscape of the coast (Jefferson Davis's Beauvoir mansion in Biloxi still flies a Confederate flag), it doesn't dominate the Gulf Coast. Ward agrees that, in some way, her characters were responding to being out of their cultural element.

On the drive from Pass Christian to Ward's hometown of DeLisle and a spot that is her source of inspiration, I can see how intimately she feels connected to this landscape; the setting she takes me to matches a description from her memoir *Men We Reaped*: "DeLisle hugs the back of the Bay of St. Louis before spreading away and thinning further upcountry." When we arrive at Ward's favorite spot, I see a grove of live oak trees, heavily covered in moss, right beside the historic marker for the town of DeLisle. It is also the spot where Ward has asked to have her marker placed on the Mississippi Writers Trail. While under the trees and looking out at the bayou, I asked Ward if she ever thinks she could leave Mississippi. "Emotionally, it's very difficult for me to leave this place, even though logically I know that leaving might probably be better for me. This place helps me keep a sense of urgency in my work." Of her children and the decision she has made to raise them in the coastal town of DeLisle, she said, "I hope that at least one of them will want to remain here in this place that I love more than I loathe, and I hope the work that I have done to make Mississippi a place worth living is enough."

IN A 1971 LECTURE, Ralph Ellison cited Heraclitus's axiom, "Geography is fate," in comparing how the way his native Oklahoma shaped him was different from the way Mississippi shaped Richard Wright. Although reinvention and renewal represent part of the artistic vision of the work of Trethewey and Ward, both writers have been uniquely shaped by their geographic origins and surrounding landscape. Geography is both fate and literary inspiration. Natasha Trethewey and Jesmyn Ward are two writers who represent the future of Mississippi and Southern letters while maintaining a firm link to the past. Both writers weave stories—one in poetry, the other in prose—about people marginalized and forgotten. But what connects them is that they have both chosen to memorialize the Southern past, one that many would rather forget than remember.

The Southern past these two writers explore is one they have defined on their own terms rather than within the proscribed boundaries of Southernness and the idea of Southern exceptionalism. The Mississippi they write about is not one that glosses over the state's sometimes tortured history. Trethewey has chosen to use memory to explore the personal and historical South, and Ward is willing to wrestle with the state's twin demons of race and poverty in her fiction.

The American idea of blackness—not merely as a racialized category, but as a cultural, political, and economic identity—has its origins in the American South. In the work of Trethewey and Ward we see how blackness at its very root is American. They also help us see

how trauma lies at the root of blackness and why that trauma must be confronted rather than buried or pushed aside. It is only by facing the impact of the psychic wounds inflicted by Mississippi in the art of these writers that Mississippi and America can begin to reckon with the past.

For both Trethewey and Ward, the Gulf Coast is a place that is as much a part of them as it is an inspiration for their art. This is especially true for Jesmyn Ward. As Ward and I stood under those large live oak trees in DeLisle that afternoon, a sudden silence fell over our conversation.

The towering live oak trees in Jesmyn Ward's hometown of Delisle
are among the largest and oldest on the Gulf Coast.

With a tone of urgency punching the quiet, Ward asked me if I detected
an eggy, sulphurous smell coming from the Bayou. I breathed it in and
responded with a quiet yes. It is a smell that makes her think of home,
she told me. Then she asked me to stand still. "Feel that warm air around
you," Ward said with a gentle lilt of serenity in her voice. "It feels as if the
air is touching you here. The humidity is like a warm embrace. I find it
hard to leave that."

CHAMELEON SEA AND WHITE SAND

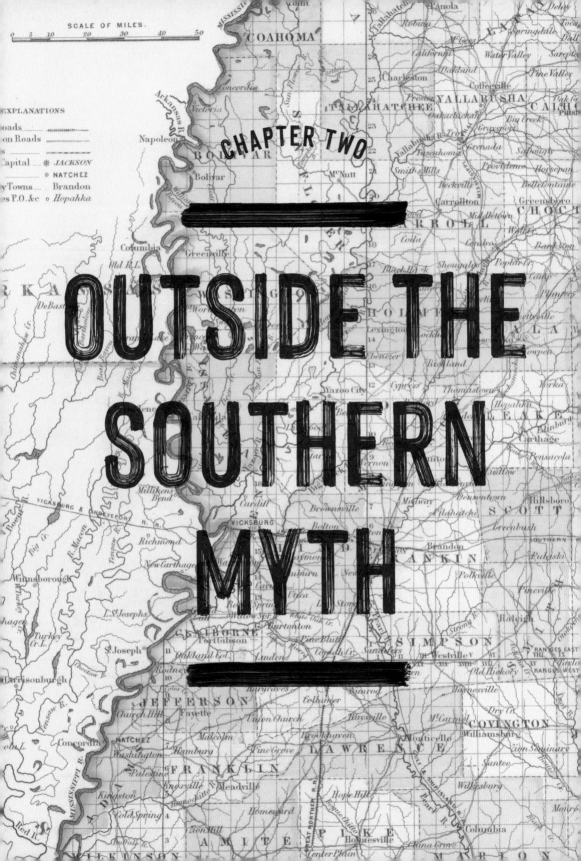

CHAPTER TWO

OUTSIDE THE SOUTHERN MYTH

In the southern Mississippi swamp you can watch the world awaken as the pale yellow sun edges itself between the trees and moss and widewinged cranes.

—Michael Farris Smith, *Desperation Road*

ON THE TRIP NORTH from the coastal lands of Mississippi—with their beaches and creole-influenced culture—the landscape and sensibility of the state begins to change. It's something Michael Farris Smith's characters notice as they trudge along Interstate 55 toward the south Mississippi town of McComb in *Desperation Road*: Even in the dead of winter, south Mississippi awakes with a hint of green. That green remains prominent in the southern part of the state because of the vast pine forests that blanket the region, a sign you have entered the Piney Woods. Once a dense forest, the Piney Woods are part of a broad coastal plain that stretches from southern Virginia to East Texas.

In 1862 historian J. F. H. Claiborne wrote in *Harper's* that Mississippi's Piney Woods was a place that "sustains a magnificent pine forest, capable of supplying for centuries to come the navies of the world." Claiborne even wondered if the Piney Woods was the location of the miraculous fountain sought out by Ponce de León in the sixteenth century. In the late nineteenth and early twentieth centuries logging took whole swaths of the Piney Woods, leaving behind what you see today: a prairie land of softly rolling hills dotted with pine trees. Mississippi's Works Progress Administration *WPA Guide* only devotes one paragraph to this region of the state, noting that the Piney Woods "is a rather haphazard and irregular triangle, whose scenery of stumps, ghost lumber towns, and hastily reforested areas tells its saga."

While logging is no longer the dominant industry of the Piney Woods, it is stamped on the region's identity. Logging yards can still be found on remote rural roads, and the once-booming rural communities that revolved around the logging industry are not yet ghost towns but hang on, evidence of the scrappy survival instincts of the people. This is a part of the state that sought to remake itself after the Civil War, with lots of tidy little towns that sprang up along new railroad lines. These were Southern spaces, though not the same Southern spaces as defined by the rest of the state. Much of the Piney Woods was essentially frontier well into the twentieth century, which has led many to see this part of the state as a place where not much happened.

Piney Woods native and Thurber Prize–winning humorist Harrison Scott Key sees the Piney Woods as an area that is hard for many Mississippians to describe. "We have few great battles, no particular music, and only a handful of notable residents from the last hundred years. Most folks from the Piney Woods have claimed—or been claimed by—these other regions, due to their cultural magnetism, I think. It's hard

Pine logs stacked on trucks like matchsticks are still
a common sight in the Piney Woods.

45

A sunrise over the De Soto National Forest, which covers ten counties in Mississippi's Piney Woods.

telling people you're from that part of Mississippi. I just tell people I'm from the bush."

As a Piney Woods native, I don't think of this land as being remote like the untamed Australian bush nor do I see it as a haphazard landscape that is difficult to describe. The hills in this part of the state are always a lush green and they roll gently along the landscape, with the occasional setting that mimics the prairie—if the prairie were filled with tall pines. Are we known for music? Well, there are a few musicians from this part of the state, like Sterling "Mr. Satan" Magee from my hometown of Mount Olive. Born in 1936, he grew up attending a Baptist church and worried his mother when he discovered the blues, known throughout the South as the devil's music. Magee—Mr. Satan to his friends—may be the best-known bluesman from this region, even though he made his mark as a musician and artist on the streets of Harlem. As a family friend who has lived in the

A gently rolling field outside of Mount Olive.

region for all of his ninety-three years told me, this is a place that more than anything is known for holding on to its frontier origins, which means that there are large swaths of land that remain largely unchanged from the way they were in the early twentieth century. After my first trip to Ireland in my early twenties, I realized that the hills that make up the pastureland in the Piney Woods must have reminded the original frontier Scotch-Irish settlers of the homelands they left behind, particularly in the spring when the morning mist floats over the hills.

In addition to the place itself, what sustained the frontier settlers of this region was their faith. "My third dream was to make Jesus happy," Key writes in his memoir *Congratulations, Who Are You Again?* "I was a member of the Church of Christ, a nineteenth-century evangelical sect consisting of good country people who believe Satan came in the form of a piano." Although the landscape may not be haunted by antebellum spirits, it is what Flannery O'Connor would call "Christ-haunted," since it is dotted by signs promoting the power of prayer. One sign outside the tiny town of Liberty commands that "If you want God to bless America, stop legalizing sin."

Faulkner scholar Noel Polk grew up in the Piney Woods town of Picayune. It, too, was Christ-haunted; the town once had a sign at its city limits proclaiming, "Jesus is Lord over Picayune." Polk painstakingly reconstructed Faulkner's novels as he originally intended, and it was through this work that Polk began to see a difference between his South and Mississippi and that of Faulkner and other Mississippians who hailed from places with more antebellum origins, such as Natchez or Oxford. Picayune and south Mississippi, Polk said, was a place that "did not invest very much of its energies in *being Southern* in any traditional sense." South Mississippi was different from the rest of Mississippi and the South, "swaddled as we were in the tall gorgeous pines of the miles-wide strip called the Piney Woods." In the process, residents of south Mississippi "seem to have done everything we possibly could to avoid calling attention to ourselves."

Polk believes that residents of the Piney Woods grow up outside the Southern myth, "that portion of Southern history, that part of the public image of the South, that belongs to Natchez, Vicksburg, and Oxford, and that attaches itself to all the rest of us, no matter where we are from." The Piney Woods has no Civil War battlefields or courthouse squares with Civil War heroes. While many see this part of the state as just the massive pine forest between Gulfport and Jackson, much more happened in this part of Mississippi than the landscape indicates.

From the late 1930s to the early 1950s the frontier culture of the Piney Woods was captured in many of the novels and short stories of writer James Howell Street, born on October 15, 1903, in the sawmill village of Lumberton, Mississippi. His first book *Look Away!: A Dixie Notebook* included journalistic recitations of stories from his father as well as contemporary events he saw as a reporter. Street wryly remarked that his first book was called *Look Away!* and everyone did. And while his work is not very well-known today, the stories he collected are rooted in the culture and folklore of the Piney Woods and are ones that every native of the Piney Woods knows. Street said that many of the tales recounted in *Look Away!* were unpublished tales from his newspaper stories since "newspapers in the South really do not like such stories. Some of them are not pretty."

The not-so-pretty stories were matter-of-fact reports of lynchings, accounts of violence in the Scotch-Irish settlement of Sullivan's Hollow—a place *Life* magazine dubbed "the meanest valley in America"—and the story of Newt Knight, who overthrew the Confederate authorities in Jones County and raised the United States flag over the county. In time he proclaimed it to be the Free State of Jones and had a family with a former slave named Rachel, who was once owned by his grandfather. Later the story and legend of Newt Knight would become part of a five-novel

Logging has long been part of the frontier culture of Mississippi's Piney Woods. This scene outside of Ellisville in 1921 is reminiscent of James Howell Street's stories of Piney Woods logging and logging communities.

historical fiction series regarding the progress of the fictional Dabney family in the fictional Piney Woods town of Lebanon, Mississippi. The novel *Tap Roots* from that series reflects Street's attempt to create a composite character of the Piney Woods settler, more rooted in legend than in truth. Street sought to connect the anti-Confederate sentiments in the Piney Woods to the mixed-race ancestry of some residents of the region. "We can't boast of our ancestors because, when we get started talking about our families, out jumps the ghost of a pirate or a cousin of color," notes the character Sam Dabney in *Tap Roots*.

It would take historian Victoria Bynum, whose roots are in Jones County, to unravel the history of the region behind the mythology James Street created. She begins her 2001 book, *The Free State of Jones*, with the 1948 trial of Newt Knight's great-grandson Davis Knight, who was charged with the crime of miscegenation. *Tap Roots* was released as a film that same year, and this renewed interest in the Knights may have even brought attention to Davis Knight and led to his being tried and eventually acquitted for intermarriage.

In the course of her book, Bynum traces the origins and legacy of the Jones County uprising from the American Revolution to the modern civil rights movement. She takes the legend painted by James Street and compares it with the real story of the Free State of Jones and shows how a place that existed outside the Southern myth still sought to layer that mythology over itself. This approach reveals a great deal about the South's transition from slavery to segregation and gives another dimension to a region of the state that many believe lacks its own history.

ONE THING THAT MAKES the culture of Mississippi unique is that it does not have a large city that would foster the cultural trends associated with American urban life. There is nowhere with the glistening glass-and-steel ambitions of Atlanta or the old world charms of Charleston, so our urban retreats have traditionally existed outside our borders. The urban beacon in the northern part of the state sits across the Tennessee state line in Memphis, which has become a part of Mississippi because of its association with that boy from Tupelo, Elvis Presley. In the southern part of the state, New Orleans serves as the region's city, a place that holds a unique importance in the Southern imagination as much as it does in broader American culture.

The towns of the Piney Woods are rural. Yet there are towns like Hattiesburg, Laurel, and Picayune that see themselves as not being rural but not quite urban. As Noel Polk wrote in *Outside the Southern Myth*, Picayune and Hattiesburg sought to send "every pine tree . . . through its saw and planing mills, if necessary" in an effort to keep the region's rural sensibilities at a "commodified distance." Yes, money from logging did separate the residents of the towns of Picayune and Hattiesburg from their much smaller neighboring communities, many of which depended on farming. Yet neither of these towns is an urban metropolis. In *The Moviegoer*, Walker Percy captures the interstitial identity of south Mississippians when the character Binx Bolling disparages a group of women who "look like housewives from Hattiesburg" when they are hoping to get a glimpse of the actor William Holden, who is in New Orleans to make a movie. I've always thought these were not necessarily housewives—and perhaps they weren't from Hattiesburg—but Percy captured the desire of south Mississippians to identify with a more urban place than their cities would allow them to project.

South Mississippians may stand out in the more distinctively Southern environment of the Crescent City, but New Orleans is also an urban oasis that allows for the anonymity that is lacking in Mississippi towns. The cultural landscape of the two places also could not be more different. New Orleans is a city of multiple personalities that scream out for a visitor's attention and embrace. The French Quarter feels both European

New Orleans has long been a canvas upon which Mississippi
writers project their literary desires.

and Caribbean, while parts of Uptown New Orleans hold pockets of
grand and tattered Old South elegance. The towns of Piney Woods are
less schizophrenic and display a more monolithic personality and geography that feels cloaked in a desire to fit in to the landscape rather than
to stand out. Given these stark contrasts, New Orleans is also a canvas
upon which Mississippi writers, particularly those from the Piney Woods
region, project their literary desires. Perhaps New Orleans is a place
where some people of this region must go to certify their Southern-ness,
since they believe they are from a place that is not visibly Southern. And it

CHAPTER TWO

is also a place where certain things can happen that don't seem as if they could occur in Mississippi. For south Mississippians, New Orleans exists as a place that allows residents of a Christ-haunted landscape to escape from their Bible Belt mores.

Jackson-born playwright Beth Henley chose to set her some of her early plays in the Piney Woods, but for her first play in 1972, *Am I Blue?*, the setting was New Orleans. John Polk Richards, a naive college boy, from an unknown place—perhaps south Mississippi—takes a walk on the wild side of the New Orleans French Quarter with a prematurely sophisticated waif. John is waiting for his eighteenth birthday and an appointment with a New Orleans prostitute—arranged by his fraternity brothers—when he meets Ashbe, a strange sixteen-year-old girl who is stealing ashtrays. The dialogue of the play is a confessional exchange between the two characters, one that could only happen with the anonymity and freedom that New Orleans provides like a sanctuary hidden in plain sight. In a small town everyone knows your every utterance. In New Orleans there is a veil of invisibility, one these characters seek for just one evening.

Henley wrote the play after hearing the song "Am I Blue?" for the first time in a New Orleans nightclub. "I loved it immediately and helplessly," Henley writes in the introduction to her collected plays. "Whenever the bandleader asked for requests I shouted out 'Am I Blue?! Am I Blue?!' I stayed all night until the little club was empty and the small, not-really-even-all-that-good band would play that song for me one more time and then just one more again."

New Orleans was the setting for Henley's first play but she chose to set her next two plays in small Piney Woods towns. Her Pulitzer Prize-winning *Crimes of the Heart* is set in the town of Hazlehurst and *The Miss Firecracker Contest* is set in Brookhaven. Both towns rose up alongside the tracks of the old New Orleans, Jackson, and Great Northern Railroad line to New Orleans. It's almost as if the settings of her plays move northward

On May 28, 1963, Anne Moody participated in a sit-in at a Jackson Woolworth's with Joan Mulholland and John Salter Jr. Recalling the day of the sit-in in her memoir, *Coming of Age in Mississippi*, Moody wrote, "After the sit-in, all I could think of was how sick Mississippi whites were. They believed so much in the segregated Southern way of life, they would kill to preserve it."

along that old railroad line throughout her career, eventually arriving in her hometown of Jackson in her 2012 play, *The Jacksonian*.

Henley was inspired to write a play set in New Orleans from her time there, one that shows how New Orleans serves as a place of anonymous escape for Mississippians. Writer and civil rights activist Anne Moody sought to escape to New Orleans for a different reason: to get away from her impoverished existence in the small Piney Woods town of Centreville. "I went to New Orleans with the intention of getting a job as a waitress in a big time restaurant. I had been told that a waitress could make as much as fifty dollars a week, and I hoped to save three hundred dollars that summer and add it to the two hundred that was already in my bank account," Moody wrote in her 1968 book *Coming of Age in Mississippi*.

Moody was trying to escape from the plantation where her family worked and lived, in a little house that only had two rooms and a porch, as sharecroppers. "The front room next to the porch was larger than the little boxed-in kitchen you could barely turn around in," Moody wrote, bearing witness to a pre–civil rights world of poverty, threats, racism, and violence that, at the time, many outside the South did not know existed. The money Moody seeks to make in New Orleans is to fund her education and to escape her impoverished upbringing and work for civil rights.

Coming of Age in Mississippi is a book that is told in measured, eloquent anger from its very opening sentence: "I'm still haunted by dreams of the time we lived on Mr. Carter's plantation." By the time the reader accompanies Moody on her journey from her tiny sharecropper's shack to her lunch-counter protest at the Jackson Woolworth in 1963 and to her work in the civil rights movement during Freedom Summer in 1964, the terror and the beauty that were Moody's memories become imprinted on your own. Although the name Carter is a pseudonym for the owners of the farm where she grew up, the vivid description Moody gives of the rural landscape makes it easy to imagine, find, and revisit.

Today the porch-front shack where Moody grew up is gone, but the road that would have taken you past it is now named in her honor. The Anne Moody Highway moves along the rolling hills in her native Wilkinson County, past the church where she is now buried and close to the site where the shack once stood. The house had no running water, so they hauled it from a nearby pond, which rests on the landscape like an unmarked memorial to Moody's struggle in these Piney Woods hills that hold so much terrible beauty.

That terrible beauty exists in neighboring Amite County, which shaped the world of writer, preacher, and activist Will Campbell. In his book *Brother to a Dragonfly* he explains that the poor in rural Mississippi did not look at the world through the lens of happiness. "Happiness was not a part of the contract. If it came, we experienced it without naming it. If it didn't, we couldn't complain, not aware that we were due it or that it even existed." Campbell and Moody were shaped by the impoverished circumstances of their birth, but Moody was black and Campbell was white. In spite of their racial differences, Campbell would describe the two of them as being part of the same garment but just not yet sewn together. Race separated them, but they were united by growing up in poverty. Through both of these writers we see how the poor of Mississippi are separate yet connected and how they each worked to sew the pieces of an old worn fabric—the sense of Mississippi—together.

As I was writing my first book, *Ever Is a Long Time*, I read every book I could about my home state. But it was Moody's *Coming of Age in Mississippi* that left an impression. Like me, she grew up in the Piney Woods, so the landscape she described was familiar. But what still resonates in my mind was that description of her house: "We all lived in rotten wood two-room shacks."

Unlike Anne Moody, I grew up on eighty acres my family owned in a tidy brick and clapboard ranch house with polished wooden floors. My farm was a place where I had memories of feeling safe and protected in Mississippi—during the same period Moody writes so captivatingly about—while Anne Moody only felt haunted by the vulnerability of her family in the Jim Crow South. My family thrived in spite of the struggles of the civil rights era, while her family suffered economic and spiritual hardship. Moody's writing made me realize that I grew up with a measure of privilege, something I struggled to make clear in what I wrote.

As I grew up in the Piney Woods, I was exposed to the prideful poverty of people like Anne Moody's family since my father was an agricultural extension agent. What I witnessed during my 1960s Piney Woods upbringing is not too far from the description of the region in the Depression-era *WPA Guide to Mississippi*: "[Its] people are economically poor, politically unpredictable, and in a constant state of economic transition." On the many trips to far-flung farms across our county the one I remember the most is a visit to a house with visible holes in the floor, one so large that I

A tin-sided barn alongside a country road in the Piney Woods, outside Collins.

OUTSIDE THE SOUTHERN MYTH

had to walk around carefully to keep from falling to the ground beneath. Reading the words of Anne Moody, who grew up in a house like the one I visited as a boy, made that memory flood back into my consciousness.

The feudal system of tenant farming that kept people living in houses with holes in the floor is gone, yet poverty and economic desolation remain persistent issues in the Piney Woods. The reason poverty endures is because of the region's move from small farms to agribusiness and manufacturing over the past forty years. The small businesses related to family farming that kept small towns alive disappeared, as well as the idea of small family farms. The feed and seed store in my hometown of Mount Olive is now an abandoned building, a symbol of collapse that you can find in almost every town in the region. Mississippi still prides itself on being an agrarian culture built around small family farms, but that identity is based on an illusion rooted in Mississippi's past, not a present reality.

Today what were once small farms have been purchased by larger operations for expansive poultry and cattle operations. As a family friend told me on a recent visit, there are now thousand-acre plots of land owned by single farming businesses, which means that the small farmers my father once served as a county agent are rare or no longer exist. Farming exists as a business for people of means, not as a means of sustaining a family, like the farms I visited as a boy. A rural life may exist on this landscape, but it is one that is markedly different from the one that shaped me.

Now, four-lane highways bypass the small towns like my hometown of Mount Olive; the economic transition of this region is hidden behind highway exits few people take as they speed through the region. The historic Powell Drug Store in Mount Olive is a place some stop to visit, but there are few other roadside attractions. I always take the exit to Mount Olive, if only to imagine the world that existed before the current economic transition left many of the town's storefronts empty. Twenty years ago I could still see in my mind's eye the once well-tended town that existed on this

Powell Drug Store has been in business in the Piney Woods town of Mount Olive for more than a century. Originally the Calhoun Drug Company, the brick building, with its cast iron Victorian trim at street level, was constructed in 1904 and still has its original marble floor, ceilings, walls, and beloved soda fountain.

landscape and had a string of thriving small business. Today it takes more than memory to evoke a vision of what was once here.

If a storefront in Mount Olive is not empty, it is occupied by a ministry or a thrift shop. "I wish someone would come buy these buildings and start businesses in them," a resident said to me one afternoon as I took photographs. But a savior is not rising from these streets, in spite of the faith of the people who live here. Today there are only a few who remember what life in Mount Olive and other small towns once was. And those who are living in places like Mount Olive now only remember them in their decline.

Once you leave the now-empty towns and head out onto country roads, the region is lush and green. It is in the farmland of the Piney Woods that I find my literary inspiration. I can spend hours driving down those winding country roads, ones where I still remember every twist, turn, and switchback as well as how they connect through communities I visited on my county agent rounds with my father. A random mailbox or road sign may bear a familiar surname that stirs a memory but the people I knew who held those names are now gone. And so is the agrarian world of the Piney Woods that Anne Moody and I once knew, one made up of small independent farms with families who were sustained by the land. I have made my peace with that since the beauty of the place that Moody and I both remember is still there.

Holding up a mirror between what once was and what remains will most certainly be the inspiration of the next generation of writers from this region. Throughout the Piney Woods you can see elements of the past on back roads, where there are small timber operations with piles of logs stacked neatly together like matchsticks, just as they would have been a century ago. But these new timber operations are working to make room for the large cattle and poultry farms, which are carved out by shaving away the tree line to create lush green fields of grass, the seed for which is dropped by low-flying aircraft. These fields create new vistas on the land-scape for those who wander down these roads, including people like me who are looking for artistic inspiration.

On these Mississippi roads, the past and the present exist side by side. The past is there for all to see, yet perhaps is only noticeable to those who still remember it. Perhaps it is not the past Mississippi is losing on this landscape. Instead we are witnessing how the past and future are slowly becoming knitted together into one seamless garment.

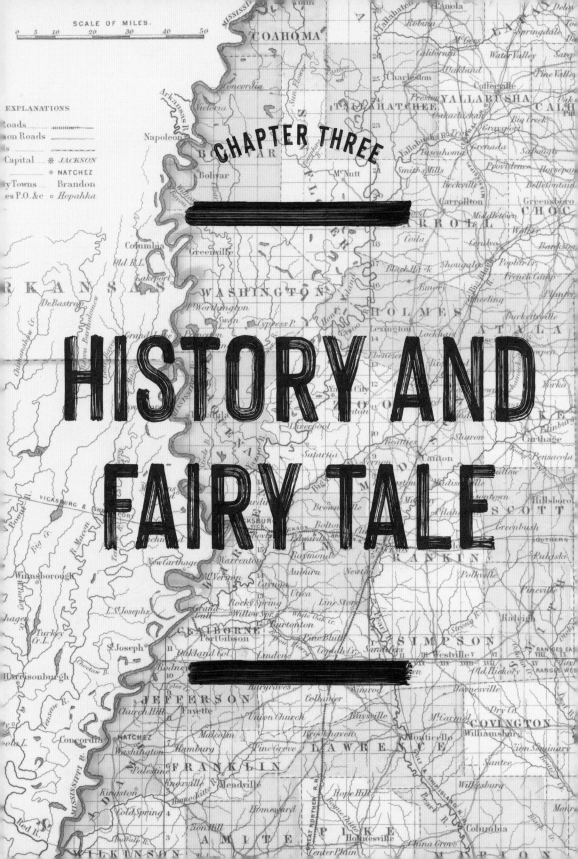

CHAPTER THREE

HISTORY AND FAIRY TALE

The line between history and fairy tale is not always clear.

—Eudora Welty, "Fairy Tale of the Natchez Trace"

NATCHEZ AND VICKSBURG both rest alongside the Mississippi. Native Americans farmed and hunted the river valleys between the two towns, and the area is home to the Emerald Mound, the largest Native American burial mound in North America. This is a landscape that was shaped as much by the native people who once inhabited it as it was by those who settled it after the land was taken from these tribes. Natchez and Vicksburg are seen more through the lens of their historical significance than their physical geography. Yet in these two historic river towns, geography may have had an impact on their destiny and history may have also played a significant role in shaping the geography.

Vicksburg is synonymous with its role in Civil War history as the place where Grant's strategy of taking control of the Mississippi River began to crush the Confederacy. The battlefield is preserved and scattered with memorials to those who fought there and Civil War enthusiasts and reenactors trek there regularly, but the town is more than a Civil War memorial. Vicksburg's Catfish Row marks the end of the Mississippi Delta and the beginning of the bluffs along the Mississippi River that drop dramatically into the river's valley.

Natchez, unlike Vicksburg, surrendered to the Union during the Civil War without a shot fired, so its nineteenth-century buildings never suffered the ravages of war. Everything seems big in Natchez, and not just the houses that were built with the spoils of the cotton kingdom by slaves.

HISTORY AND FAIRY TALE

Sunset over the Mississippi River at Natchez.

Built in 1823, Rosalie Mansion overlooks the Mississippi River and served as architectural inspiration for many of Natchez's Greek Revival mansions.

Natchez once had more wealth than any American city outside New York, and the slave market was one of the busiest in the South. Wealth and slaves in this river town in turn fed into the idea of the frontier. "Natchez remained closer to the frontier than some cared to admit," historian Harnett Thomas Kane wrote in his book *Natchez on the Mississippi*. "At Natchez were crystallized the hopes and plans of countless parties that went forth to Texas and Mexico for stealthy gain or conquest." It is also a town that historically has had a split personality, one of tranquil streets and elegant windswept heights as well as rowdy thoroughfares. At one time Natchez was a city divided: beyond the river bluffs was the town of Natchez with its elegant Greek Revival homes and then there was the region below the river bluffs known as Natchez-Under-the-Hill, a place recognized more for violence and debauchery than for elegant architecture.

Natchez was once divided by race as well as by refinement and debauchery, a division related to its position on the path toward the western frontier. Part of that path can still be followed today on the Natchez Trace. First traveled by Native Americans, the Natchez Trace played a significant role as a path for settlers to follow from the east to the Mississippi frontier. From 1785 to 1825, until the onset of steamboat travel, this dirt pathway was a popular travel passage. Today it is a national park and parkway, one lined with signs that ironically connect the stories of the Native Americans who once lived along the trail with the idea of manifest destiny that led to their removal. This is a part of Mississippi that is filled with both history and paradox, since the legend of Natchez and the Natchez Trace looms larger than the reality.

Eudora Welty was fascinated by the history and paradox of the Natchez Trace, which played a part in her story collection *The Wide Net and Other Stories*. Each of the eight stories involves travel on the Natchez Trace in one way or another, whether it is travel along the road or the consequences of that travel. Scholars of Welty's fiction, like Michael Kreyling, believe that in these stories Welty was seeking to free the Natchez Trace of its burden of history and to reimagine the landscape. That seems to be evident in the very first story in *The Wide Net*, "First Love," which is set on the Natchez Trace in 1807, a period of swift movement toward the west, one associated with "a season of dreams" and "the bitterest winter of them all." In this story the landscape is likened to the impulse of the settlers, who are described as insects whipped by the wind's "insistent penetration."

Natchez is also the birthplace of novelist Richard Wright, who saw another side of the city, which he writes about with great affection in his memoir *Black Boy*: "There was the faint, cool kiss of sensuality when dew came on to my cheeks and shins as I ran down the wet green garden paths in the early morning. . . . There was the vague sense of the infinite as I looked down upon the yellow dreaming waters of the Mississippi River from the verdant bluffs of Natchez." Wright recalls the beauty of the town of his birth after recounting how he was lashed into unconsciousness after setting his

HISTORY AND FAIRY TALE

Sunset over the Mississippi River near Vicksburg.

family's home on fire. This loving description of his hometown is bittersweet, as it was written to soften the harshness of his mistreatment as well as other painful memories. As the narrative progresses, we learn of those other painful memories, particularly how racial terrorism loomed over his family, even beside the yellow dreaming waters of the great Mississippi, a river that conjures images of beauty as much as it elicits fear.

THE MISSISSIPPI RIVER is what Bill Ferris truly connects with. It's why the work of Mark Twain is so important to him. "Twain captures the river as an actor. The river has an important role in *Huckleberry Finn*, more important than Huck and Jim." Although his farm is his favorite place in Mississippi, the river looms large for Ferris, particularly as he gazes at a photograph on the wall taken near Vicksburg's Cherry Street Bridge. "Near where that photograph was taken, there is an elegant bridge over the railroad. My grandfather used to walk me there as a child." And then there is also Fort Hill, which overlooks the river with a dramatic view, one that provides a panorama, Vicksburg on the high hill with Natchez just below it. "It's like you're sitting in the box of a theater and the stage is far below," Ferris tells me.

For more than fifty years, Bill Ferris has been documenting Mississippi and the American South not from a lofty theater box, but from the very front row. His work both updates our perspective and pays homage to

HISTORY AND FAIRY TALE

the past. In any conversation with Bill Ferris, people, place, and memory align together to create story, almost like the flow of the blues songs Ferris has spent his career documenting and studying. For someone whose life has been dedicated to legitimizing the everyday culture of the South—and seeing it as an equal to the region's literature and art—you would expect this democratic aesthetic to guide any line of inquiry. Ferris's life's work of examining the culture of the American South, particularly of his native state of Mississippi, has become imprinted on his very being. But Ferris believes that he never would have been launched on his path as a writer, scholar, and photographer without the place that shaped him: his family farm just outside of the Mississippi river town of Vicksburg.

William Reynolds Ferris was brought up on a working farm called Broadacres, about seventeen miles southeast of Vicksburg. Ferris's farm may have only had the racial binary of black and white, but the town of Vicksburg had a Jewish population, as well as Irish, Italian, Lebanese, and Chinese, many of these groups having been in the region for more than a century. "The river town—Memphis, Greenville, Vicksburg, Natchez, New Orleans—has a greater diversity of people because of the passage of people up and down the river." Although his hometown is the setting of an important Civil War battle, Ferris sees the diversity of Vicksburg as more of an influence on him than anything related to the Battle of Vicksburg.

"For me, all my work begins in Vicksburg and on the farm," Ferris told me on a spring afternoon on the campus of the University of Mississippi, in a room filled with six of his photographs hanging on the walls. "That's the deepest body of work and it's the most personal body of work because it involves the families, including my own, whom I knew from my earliest memories. Today, the faces are all gone, but they linger and are deeply etched in my memory."

What keeps them etched in Ferris's memory is that he documented those faces in photographs, many of them in bright Kodachrome color.

Bill Ferris (far left) and friends bringing in the hay on his family's farm in Vicksburg.

He began at age fourteen with a Brownie camera he got for Christmas. First, he photographed his grandmother's Christmas dinner, simply to document the meal and the moment. Then he began to photograph the people who lived on his farm. "Just a few months after getting my Brownie camera, I photographed a baptism on our farm in Hamer Bayou. And I look back on those photographs as sort of bookends of my career, trying to understand my family, but also the extended family of black families where I grew up and how all that connects."

About a dozen African Americans lived on Broadacres, and Ferris and his family worked alongside them in the fields where they raised cotton, soybeans, and cattle. As he grew older, he became interested in the music of the black church that was near their farm, Rose Hill Church. And from the gospel music he heard there, he began to see a connection with the music of blues singers he would hear on WLAC, the clear channel radio station that broadcasted across the South and could be heard in

HISTORY AND FAIRY TALE

The congregation of Rose Hill Church in Warren County, 1975. It was here that Ferris recorded Reverend Isaac Thomas's sermons that he later transcribed into poetic stanzas.

NEXT SPREAD: In his photographs, Ferris documented Mississippi's people as well as its vernacular architecture, like in this 1975 image of S.M. White & Son Crossroads Store on Old Port Gibson Road, Reganton.

twenty states. From blues and gospel, he began to connect the music to the oral tradition, and he witnessed how stories were told by the men and women who worked with him on the farm. Then he began to see the camera in a more focused way. "I began to understand photography as a kind of expression that had more than just what my heart led me to. It was an artistic documentary voice."

Bill Ferris's photographs explore an idea that has been at work in the American South since post-Reconstruction: the idea of a new South, one based on industrial development rather than cotton, and moderation on issues with respect to race. Folklore and myth are the twin pillars of Southern culture, and the idea of a new South was one way to push the mythical South to the side. By the 1970s, when the idea of a new South came up again, it was in light of changes brought about by the civil rights movement.

In his seminal book *The Mind of the South*, W. J. Cash said that the South is "not quite a nation within a nation but the next thing to it." What Ferris's photographs do is capture Mississippi at a particular moment—during and after the civil rights revolution and what historian C. Vann Woodward calls "the Bulldozer Revolution," which chipped away at the South's predominantly agrarian way of life—and they make us explore questions of the persistence of the idea of Southern distinctiveness.

This idea of Southern distinctiveness was one Ferris soon discovered when he explored the work of Walker Evans and Frederic Ramsey Jr., both of whom had photographed places around Mississippi and in the town of Vicksburg. Ramsey's book *Been Here and Gone*, which documents black vernacular life and music in the South, was one Ferris stumbled across as a student at Davidson College. *Been Here and Gone* made Ferris realize that the place where he was from had a culture that was of interest to the rest of the world. "In the same way that Alan and John Lomax's recordings for the Library of Congress of Mississippi blues singers and inmates at Parchman penitentiary singing work songs, I was doing similar recordings and

HISTORY AND FAIRY TALE

photographs on my farm. I saw that as a sort of affirmation of what I was doing by people who were famous in places like the Library of Congress and who published their work in books of photographs."

Throughout Ferris's academic career, he has given a lecture that serves as a primer on Southern studies called "Memory and Place in the American South" that draws on some of these photographs and experiences. While he is proud of his books, including *Blues from the Delta*, *Local Color*, and his work on the first *Encyclopedia of Southern Culture*, Ferris believes that his ideas and writing about place and memory all spring from his photography work, which began on his farm south of Vicksburg. "Photographs, I now realize, more than any other medium, capture memory and sense of place for all people. And there's no home you can enter that does not have photographs on tables and walls that capture the people, and places, and the memory of family and community that is most personal for whoever lives in that house."

For Bill Ferris, photography is a narrative form. "There is a story lurking, if not in full view, in every photograph. And there are narratives that emerge when you place a group of photographs together on a table." It's what Ferris confronted when he was sequencing images for his book *The South in Color*, the third volume in his trilogy on the American South (the other books are *Give My Poor Heart Ease: Voices of the Mississippi Blues* and *The Storied South: Voices of Writers and Artists*). He began to see which photographs did not tell the best story and how certain images, when grouped together, told a more compelling one. It's something he also learned from his friend, fellow Mississippi writer Eudora Welty, who he sees as an influence on his work. "Eudora would tell a story about individual images of people. In some cases, they actually connected to her fiction." Ferris said that is especially true of Welty's famous photograph "A Woman of the Thirties," which served as the inspiration for her character Phoenix Jackson in her short story "A Worn Path."

Ferris has even used photography in helping to collect oral history. It's what he did when he interviewed mule and horse trader Ray Lum, when he was trying to get Lum to tell his stories of auctioneers and a time of farming in the South before the advent of the tractor. Lum was in his eighties and Ferris was in his twenties when he interviewed him, and Ferris found it challenging to ask Lum what life was like for him as a child. So to prime the pump of Lum's memories, Ferris tracked down photographs of Lum's young life and the world he would have known then. "I could lay those in front of him and he could talk for hours not just about the photographs but about the associations of memory. And many of the richest bodies of narration I got from Ray Lum were in response to photographs from his family album and from historic photographs of mules, horses, and traders, some of the cockney traders in England. And no matter where I went to find photographs, they would trigger his memory."

The result of Ferris's work with Lum was the book "*You Live and Learn. Then You Die and Forget it All*": *Ray Lum's Tales of Horses, Mules, and Men.* While it may be thought of as a work of oral history, it is a heavily descriptive narrative not just of Lum's life as a livestock trader and auctioneer,

but also of the place and setting that shaped Lum's life. Ferris may have used photographs to elicit stories for Ray Lum to tell him, but he also used those same photographs to give the reader a sense of place in the narrative. Lum's greatest fear was that when he died, all of his stories would

In his stories of mule and horse trading captured by Ferris, Ray Lum (1871–1977) left behind an important record of Mississippi's oral storytelling tradition.

HISTORY AND FAIRY TALE

go with him. Ferris not only preserved the stories, but also helped us see the world that helped create them.

One of Ferris's great strengths is capturing the voices of the people he encounters in his oral history and documentary work. It's another part of his toolkit as a folklorist that was shaped by his farm. "When you grow up in a place like I did—an isolated farm—the voices you know best are the voices that live there. And that would be my family and the black families who also lived on our farm. They both spoke different styles of English. And I understood and could speak them both." Ferris's linguistic fluidity is a part of his Grammy-winning book, music, and spoken word compilation *Voices of Mississippi*. If you listen to the songs and stories, they follow the cadence of the time and place they came from, both in terms of sound and on the page. "I labored many hours over the transcriptions that are in the book. Because I see that as oral literature written down in ways that allow you to look at, say, Reverend Isaac Thomas's sermon as poetry."

That is exactly how the sermon appears on the page. Ferris took Reverend Thomas's delivery and placed it on the page in five stanzas that correspond to the pauses in the way the sermon is delivered. And it is hard not to listen and imagine yourself sitting in the pews of Rose Hill Church in 1968, clapping your hands to the rhythm of the delivery of the sermon and cooling yourself down with a cardboard fan emblazoned with the name of the local funeral home.

While he was directing the Center for the Study of Southern Culture at the University of Mississippi (the first center devoted to the academic study of the region) and during his time at the University of North Carolina, Ferris taught a class on Southern literature in the oral tradition. The premise of the class was that Southern writers such as Richard Wright, William Faulkner, Tennessee Williams, and Alice Walker all were astute listeners, and they transformed the stories they heard into fiction, poetry, or drama. "And therein lies the power of what the human voice is all about: either the oral performance of speech or the written, artistic rendering of a work of art."

Which made me wonder, will Mississippi's oral tradition remain the same in the digital age? Is Mississippi maintaining or losing its oral tradition? "I think of the oral tradition as you might think of the Mississippi River," Ferris said. "You can never step in the same water twice. It's constantly changing." Ferris thinks there is still power left in Mississippi's voices today. Of course, the voices will change from generation to generation, but Mississippi's current generation of storytellers are heirs to the older forms of oral tradition and storytelling. "The mule trader era died out with the coming of automobiles and tractors. But those voices continued as used car salesmen who talked about horsepower and talked in loving ways about automobiles and tractors as the mule trader had talked about horses and mules," Ferris said with a grin. "So, there will be change, but the power of oral tradition, I think, will always be given in all life, but in a place like Mississippi it will be especially important."

Because of Ferris's close perspective and tight focus on what was important about Mississippi's culture, as well as the South writ large, we know how the new South and the old South intersect. And that is exactly what Ferris wants his readers to see and learn and continue to explore.

IF BILL FERRIS LAYERS NARRATIVE over his work as a folklorist and photographer, Greg Iles links the folklore and reality of place together tightly within the thousands of pages of his books, including his Natchez Burning trilogy. Some might label Iles's writing as Southern gothic, with its mixture of secrets, race, and violence, but the tight narratives of his thrillers are much more than that. Iles uses the setting of his hometown of Natchez not just as a gothic backdrop and a means of getting to deeper issues of race but also as a way to explore Southern memory and forgetting.

HISTORY AND FAIRY TALE

The past looms large in Iles's novels, but the past also serves as a window into the present.

Like Natchez native Richard Wright, Iles feels a sensual connection to this river town where he has lived since the age of three. "The tactile, hyper-vivid impressions of childhood imprint themselves more deeply upon us than anything except possibly smells or sound or music," Iles told me. Though his memories of the river and the geography of Natchez match those of Wright, Iles feels that is where the similarities between them end. "For me Natchez was a dreamlike cocoon of safety and mostly positive experience," Iles remembers and then quickly turns to the difference. "Wright would learn very young that it was something altogether different for him. How many young black children experienced those pure joys, only to have them tainted, then ruined by the realization that they had been born the 'wrong' color? All of them."

Greg Iles's family arrived in Natchez in December 1963 after his father served as an army physician in Germany. That year also marked the height of the civil rights movement in Mississippi. The marches and demonstrations that could be found in towns like Jackson and McComb came to Iles's hometown late in the movement but are mirrored by the drama and violence in his fiction. In 1965, the near-fatal car bombing of NAACP president George Metcalfe led to a boycott of white-owned businesses. Violence returned in 1967 when NAACP member Wharlest Jackson Sr. was killed in a car bombing after being promoted to a job once open only to whites at a local tire factory. So, in addition to the beauty of his hometown, Greg Iles grew up with violence as a backdrop to his childhood, violence he learned later in life was connected with the racial legacy of his Natchez.

There is little doubt about the setting of Iles's fiction, since he uses physical detail to place the reader in his hometown of Natchez. His novel *Turning Angel* is named after a statue in the city cemetery that seems to

Demonstrators run down the street in Natchez in 1967 after a report that white youths with a gun were nearby.

turn around and follow you with her eyes, and *The Devil's Punchbowl* was named after a ravine below the same cemetery. Iles's Natchez books are, by design, very careful blends of authentic and fictional places. "Many people from this area love reading my books because so many actual places appear in them, sometimes as settings for set-piece scenes. It's the same with the history of the town. I try to blend my created past with the actual past so inextricably that even historians will have difficulty unraveling truth from fiction." Iles's Natchez is a combination of the real and the imagined. And while the characters of Penn Cage, Tom Cage, Caitlin Masters, Sheriff Billy Byrd, and many others in his trilogy of thrillers are fictional, Iles's use of actual places in the town of Natchez provides a lifelike backdrop to his characters' lives and makes them feel real.

When you visit Natchez, you even expect to encounter Iles's fictionalized personalities walking down the street beside you. With respect to the created landscape of his fiction, Iles told me, "I'm very proud of the town of Bienville, Mississippi, which I created in my most recent novel,

Cemetery Road. It feels so real that I'm worried that people will come here from France or Australia to explore it. When I first sat down to write as a 31-year-old musician, I could not have imagined that effect."

Iles turned to writing fiction after several years on the road as a guitarist, vocalist, and songwriter with his band Frankly Scarlet. After he quit the band in 1989, he gave himself one year to write and sell a novel. That was his

The turning angel statue in the Natchez City Cemetery.

first thriller, the World War II–era novel *Spandau Phoenix*. It was not until he wrote his first novel featuring the character Penn Cage, *The Quiet Game*, that he began to use Natchez as a setting. *The Quiet Game* was a bit of a valentine to his hometown. Penn is just arriving back home from Houston and finds himself rediscovering the place where he grew up. Then Penn begins to dig deeper into the history of Natchez.

"When I wrote *The Quiet Game*, I didn't want—or wasn't yet ready—to simply tell the story of the civil rights killing that inspired the novel's central murder. Because that kind of murder is actually brutally simple, and at that age I felt it was fundamentally uninteresting from a crime fiction point of view. Similarly, a novel about unrepentant Nazis would be a pretty boring tale of murder. So, I wrote a more complex tale." Iles said that as he grew older and wiser, he came to know about several race murders near his hometown that had a much more complex origin. These were "murders of 'everyday' black folks, by which I mean non-activists. These were carried out by a hyper-violent offshoot of the Ku Klux Klan, one that had been far more effective than the Klan at spreading terror in my region. By this time in life, I had also learned a lot more about the hidden lives of the men who had led my community for years, even generations. All these hidden truths cried out to be explored."

And that is what Iles does in his Natchez Burning trilogy. In *Natchez Burning*, the first in the trio of thrillers that takes readers back fifty years to chilling civil rights–era murders and conspiracies in Iles's hometown, he uses place and history to set the scene:

> Let us begin in 1964, with three murders. Three stones cast into a pond no one had cared about since the siege of Vicksburg, but which was soon to become the center of the world's attention. A place most people in the United States like to think was somehow different from the rest of the country, but which was in fact the very incarnation of America's tortured soul.
>
> Mississippi.

Natchez Burning derives its title from the famous Howlin' Wolf song about the tragic Rhythm Club fire in Natchez in 1940. While the novel does not deal with that fire, the victim of the first murder that takes place in the novel is singing that song to pass the time just before he is killed.

Blues songs and Mississippi both function as characters in Iles's fiction, and Iles continues to draw from the historical for the character Caitlin Masters, a journalist in *Natchez Burning*. Stanley Nelson, editor of the *Concordia Sentinel* in Ferriday, Louisiana—just eleven miles from Natchez—served as the inspiration for Masters, who is fixated on solving the civil rights–era murder of a black music shop owner. Similarly, Nelson

HISTORY AND FAIRY TALE

tackled the cold case of the murder of Frank Morris, who was killed when his shoe shop was set on fire in 1964.

Nelson was nine years old when the Ku Klux Klan torched Frank Morris's business shortly after midnight on December 10, 1964, but the story came to haunt him in adulthood. Morris had been asleep in the back of his shoe shop when he heard glass breaking and saw two men pouring gasoline outside the building. Morris died four days after he emerged from the back of his shop completely in flames, leaving behind a trail of bloody footprints. Beginning in 2007, it took Stanley Nelson four years and 150 stories published in his newspaper before a grand jury was convened to investigate the murder. The suspect Nelson named, Leonard Spencer, was brought to Nelson's attention by Spencer's own family.

Similarly, in *Natchez Burning* the character Penn Cage is forced to defend his idolized father—Tom Cage, the city's beloved doctor—when he is accused of murdering his African American nurse. Someone once described his book *Natchez Burning* as what would happen if Jem Finch from *To Kill A Mockingbird* learned things about his father, Atticus, that no boy should know. Through the three books in Iles's trilogy—*Natchez Burning*, *The Bone Tree*, and *Mississippi Blood*—he uses his hometown as a means of examining how race and place shape American identity. "All my books are an inquiry into the nature of evil," Iles told an NPR interviewer in 2014 after the release of *Natchez Burning*. "Why do good people do bad things? Are any human beings completely evil? Do we all have good within us? That's what I'm interested in."

Iles tends to write in a very granular way with a great deal of detail and history as part of the narrative. The Natchez Burning trilogy is over two thousand pages long, yet the action occurs over a mere five or six days, not counting flashbacks. So, in addition to his connection to the landscape of Natchez and getting his details right, he has also become obsessed with the fluid nature of time on the page.

In talking about time, our discussion came to the role of memory in Iles's writing. How much of his landscape is drawn from memory and does he fact check his memory? "Memory is the raw material of the writer's craft. Should it be fact-checked? In most cases no, unless the writer is pursuing a polemical objective." Iles then quotes his friend and bandmate Stephen King from the Rock Bottom Remainders, a group of writers who perform together: "Kids, fiction is the truth inside the lie, and the truth of fiction is simple: the magic exists." Iles believes that writers have a special relationship with their memories, or the way they access and process them. "Therein may lie a clue to what separates novelists from other people," Iles concludes.

There are many phrases that describe his hometown of Natchez and the South, but one stands out for Iles. It was written by journalist Marshall Frady in *Dixie Rising*: "In the South, the Old Testament and the Crucifixion always seemed to count for more than the New Testament and the Resurrection." Turning the other cheek, even in the heart of the Bible belt, rarely happens in the real or imagined world of Mississippi; justice is an eye for an eye.

For Iles, the river town of Natchez embodies the unforgiving ways of the river that runs alongside it. As Mark Twain wrote in *Life on the Mississippi*, "One who knows the Mississippi will promptly aver—not aloud, but to himself—that ten thousand River Commissions, with the mines of the world at their back, cannot tame that lawless stream, cannot curb it or confine it, cannot say to it, 'Go here,' or 'Go there,' and make it obey; cannot save a shore which it has sentenced; cannot bar its path with an obstruction which it will not tear down, dance over, and laugh at." Natchez and the Mississippi may look idyllic and romantic, but what Greg Iles seeks to find in his fiction is the darkness that lies beneath the glamor and the light. And in that darkness lies a glimmer of the reality of the place.

As Iles told me about the role of landscape in his work, "I write of the Mississippi having a physical power not easily quantified or even described, like a separate center of gravity—spiritual gravity—that pulls constantly on all who live near it. Even when you can't see the river, you sense it out there through the trees, below the bluffs, dividing the very nation. What is the nature of that power? Destructive? Purging? Blessing in what it brings us every year, for the most part. All I know is, the river is part of me, and I am of the river. And its name is Mississippi."

Mississippi's chroniclers of these two river towns both try to examine them free of the mythology that tends to envelop them, particularly as it relates to their historic connection to the Civil War. Bill Ferris uses his family farm near Vicksburg rather than the battlefields nearby as the launching point for his life's work of documenting the music, art, and stories of Mississippi and the American South, whether it is blues and gospel or the stories of former livestock and mule traders. Novelist Greg Iles uses his hometown of Natchez—a place he describes as a nineteenth-century town preserved in amber—to explore issues of race and family in the South. Ferris and Iles create in vastly different genres, but their work is firmly rooted in the towns that shaped them.

CHAPTER THREE

"All I know is, the river is part of me, and I am of the river. And its name is Mississippi."

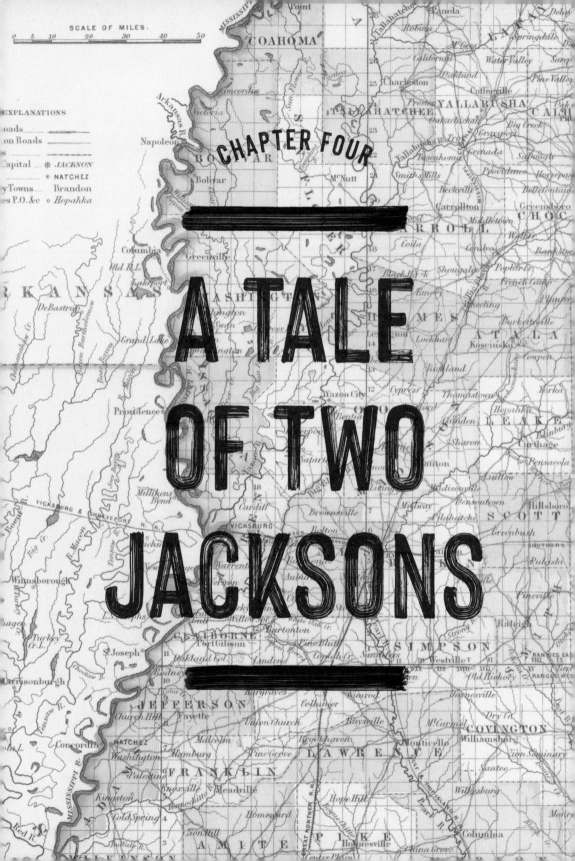

CHAPTER FOUR

A TALE OF TWO JACKSONS

I knew you and Grandmama were safer back in Jackson than I was up north. . . . Y'all were safer because you knew exactly where you were in the world.

—Kiese Laymon, *Heavy: An American Memoir*

*E*AST OF VICKSBURG, in the center of Mississippi's capital city of Jackson, stands a building of white stone with a commanding clock tower bearing a gleaming lavender face. If you look closely you can see gargoyles peering over the building's upper edges. When the building first opened, upside-down alligator sculptures greeted visitors at street level but they have since disappeared, victims of renovations and changing tastes.

Built in the Gothic Revival style, the Lamar Life Building bears a slight resemblance to New York's Woolworth Building in appearance though not in height—it is only ten stories tall. When it was completed in 1925, it was the first skyscraper in what was a growing city on the edge of Mississippi's red clay hills and at the time was the largest office building in the state. The clock tower was even once known as the Singing Tower because it housed a radio station. That clock tower, for me, has come to symbolize the meeting of literary minds from the past and present in Jackson. Of writers who wrote of and were inspired by pre–civil rights Jackson, and of writers who know a post-integration city.

In 1924, a man by the name of Christian Webb Welty had climbed the corporate ladder at the Lamar Life Insurance Company to become its general manager and vice president. He also had the responsibility of overseeing the construction of the new headquarters. His daughter clearly took great pride in her father's project and spent time in the building as it began to command a presence over downtown Jackson. "At

When it was completed in 1925, the Lamar Life Building
was the first skyscraper in Mississippi.

every stage of the building, Daddy took his family to see as much as we could climb over, usually on Sunday mornings," she recalled when looking back on her life. "At last we could climb by the fire escape to reach the top. We stood on the roof, with the not-yet-working clock tower at our backs, and viewed all Jackson below, spread to its seeable limits, its green rim, where the still river-like Pearl River and the still-unpaved-over Town Creek meandered and joined together in their unmolested swamp, with

Downtown Jackson, with the state capitol in the foreground.

Eudora Welty wrote most of her stories and novels from the upstairs bedroom of this house on Pinehurst Street in Jackson's Belhaven neighborhood.

'the country' beyond. We were located where we stood there—part of our own map."

The family once lived nearby in a yellow two-story house at 741 North Congress Street—the same street on which, in roughly thirty years, Mississippi-born writer Richard Ford would live as well. During the construction of the Lamar Life Building, the Welty family moved to Belhaven, one of Jackson's first suburbs. Christian Welty enlisted the Lamar Life Building's architect to design a home for his family on Pinehurst Street. That Tudor-style house on Pinehurst also became the lifelong home of Christian Welty's daughter, the writer Eudora Welty, who recalled the journey to the clock tower under construction in her memoir *One Writer's*

Beginnings. Welty, like her fellow North Congress Street denizen Richard Ford, would be awarded the Pulitzer Prize in Literature.

It is the house on Pinehurst Street where Welty wrote most of her stories and novels. Inside the house, books can be found on nearly every surface, much as they could when Welty lived there. Outside, the gardens have been restored to the original design used by Welty's mother, Chestina, who planned the garden so that something was in bloom in every season. When you walk inside the house, it almost seems as if Eudora Welty has just stepped out for a moment and will soon return to greet you properly.

Although Welty did most of her writing in an upstairs bedroom of this house, her source of literary inspiration was the land and people of Mississippi. She not only drew on settings that she knew of from her native Jackson but also found inspiration from her travels around the state, particularly while she worked for the Works Progress Administration in the 1930s. There are few corners of Mississippi Welty did not visit during her WPA travels, so in many ways the entire state served as her literary canvas. Several of those places were captured in her photographs, which are as much a part of her literary legacy as her stories and novels.

Eudora Welty used photography to create an intersection of fictional narrative, personal memory, and the region's historical past. As a photographer, Welty very much believed in direct documentation of human behavior, particularly in having a connection with her subject or a place. But it was place that was most important to Welty. "Like a good many writers . . . I am myself touched off by place," she wrote in her 1955 essay in the *Virginia Quarterly Review* "How I Write." "Place opens a door in the mind." So it would follow that place and setting, which are key in her fiction, would also become part of her photography and that the two might intersect in a character in her work.

That character was one of Welty's most memorable: Phoenix Jackson in "A Worn Path." In this story Welty narrates the long winter's journey of

9 9

It is hard to look at Eudora Welty's photograph, "A Woman of the Thirties," and not think about her character Phoenix Jackson from her short story "A Worn Path."

a "very old and small" African American woman named Phoenix Jackson who is seeking medicine to help her ailing grandson. Welty describes Phoenix as a woman who "looked straight ahead. Her eyes were blue with age. Her skin had a pattern all its own of numberless branching wrinkles and as though a whole little tree stood in the middle of her forehead, but a golden color ran underneath." It is hard not to look at Welty's photograph "A Woman of the Thirties" and see Phoenix, right down to the "branching wrinkles" in the middle of her forehead. With her coat securely buttoned, she looks as if she is at the beginning of a long walk, much like the character in "A Worn Path."

"A Worn Path" is a story rich in description and setting, but it is also one that holds a mirror up to the power dynamic at work against Phoenix. Phoenix Jackson is viewed as a "charity case" by both the white medical service professionals with whom she interacts and the white hunter she encounters in the woods on her way into town to obtain the medication. Throughout the story, Welty finds ways to quietly remind the reader of the history of structural injustice that has determined Phoenix's social and economic position and placed her on the worn path of her journey down a deserted country road in Mississippi.

In a single photograph Welty had found the core of a story, the beginning of a narrative. Welty's photographs of Mississippi reveal the wide-ranging curiosity and unstinting empathy that also marks her work as a writer. Her photographs are usually in outdoor settings and the landscape is as much a part of the image as the person or object she caught in the frame. Welty's photographs evoke memories of a time when Mississippi was a much more insular place, with unique hand-lettered signs rather than the mass-produced ones that are now ubiquitous all over the country. And because Welty as a photographer was so engaged with her subjects, she often engaged in conversation with the people she photographed before clicking the shutter of her camera and kept in touch with many of

A TALE OF TWO JACKSONS

In her photographs, Eudora Welty captured life in Mississippi during the
1930s, as she did here at the Mississippi State Fair in 1939.

them. Her photographic subjects project a degree of trust simply because their expressions and body language seem genuine and not posed.

Many see a link between Welty and the photographers of the Farm Security Administration (FSA), such as Dorothea Lange, Marion Post Wolcott, and Walker Evans, photographers who skillfully captured poverty and race in the American South. But that connection fits only chronologically rather than by method. FSA photographers, particularly Walker

Before the Civil War, Windsor Plantation was the largest private residence in Mississippi, with twenty-nine Corinthian columns each 45 feet tall. In 1890, a fire destroyed the home. When Eudora Welty photographed the ruins in 1942 during a picnic there with friends—her shadow can be seen in the foreground of this image—only twenty-three columns remained.

Evans, composed their images with a sense of detachment. For Eudora Welty, detaching herself from the place and people of her home was impossible. Photography for Welty was all about what she felt, both about the place or the people she photographed.

American poet Diane Ackerman wrote that to "understand the world," whether it is the world of the South, love, art, or war, whether particular to one place or time or of any or all time, one must "first detect it through the radar net of our senses." For Welty, it was the job of the writer to present, "steadily visible from its outside, . . . a continuous, shapely, pleasing and furnished surface to the eye. . . . Indeed, great fiction shows us not how to conduct our behavior but how to feel."

If you walk around Eudora Welty's Jackson neighborhood, you can still get a sense of the world she inhabited, though it is no longer as self-contained a place as it was during her early years. The Belhaven neighborhood is still quiet and sometimes you can hear music floating through the air from Belhaven University, spilling out of the same building that inspired Welty to write her story "June Recital." The Lamar Life Building is undergoing yet another transformation, from office building to downtown loft apartments, a sign that the country town Welty once knew now views itself through a more urban lens. But Welty would still recognize the lavender clock tower she visited as a child and the building where she once worked as a copywriter for the radio station, one of her first paying jobs as a writer. Welty saw change as inevitable, but she liked capturing moments and freezing them in time in her photographs so that she could revisit them, whether in her fiction or just to remember. "It is our inward journey that leads us through time—forward or back, seldom in a straight line, most often spiraling," she wrote in *One Writer's Beginnings*. "Each of us is moving, changing, with respect to others. As we discover, we remember; remembering, we discover; and most intensely do we experience this when our separate journeys converge. Our living

Belhaven University sits across the street from Eudora Welty's house and was where Welty said she heard "the recurring dreams of youth" echoing from the music department.

experience at those meeting points is one of the charged dramatic fields of fiction."

The west side of Jackson feels separate and distinct from the wooded streets and trimmed lawns of Belhaven, a legacy of years of segregation that once divided this city. In the 1920s, black people could only live on the west side of Capitol Street, north of the black business district on Farish Street, and on the southwest side in a few new communities. Jim Hill High School can be found in the heart of West Jackson on Lynch Street. The school is named after a man who rose to become the first black speaker of the Mississippi House of Representatives and who was one of the first black men to serve in Congress during Reconstruction. Jim Hill students

A TALE OF TWO JACKSONS

ABOVE Jackson's Farish Street in the 1940s. BELOW The Alamo
Theater, restored in the 1990s, on Farish Street today.

are told about this history as well as the school's involvement with the civil rights movement, including how the school joined Anne Moody and students from nearby Tougaloo College in a sit-in protest at a downtown Woolworth. They are also told about a writer who attended Jim Hill back when it was an elementary school, before the promise and hope of the Great Migration lured this writer away to Chicago. His name was Richard Nathaniel Wright.

Although he was born in Natchez, part of Wright's formative years, before leaving for the North, were spent in West Jackson. It is his education in Jackson at Jim Hill that provided the groundwork for his self-education after he left Mississippi. Outside of his memoir *Black Boy* and his novel *The Long Dream*, little of Wright's work is set in his home state. But it is in Mississippi and around the environs of Jim Hill that Wright encountered the theme that would propel his literary career: hunger.

Even the epigraph Wright placed in *Black Boy* alludes to hunger. It is taken from the Book of Job in the Old Testament: "His strength shall be hunger-bitten, / And destruction shall be ready at his side." The epigraph tells the reader that hunger would be Wright's Job-like struggle, the one that would endure for the course of his life. For Richard Wright, physical and psychic starvation were as much a part of his childhood in Mississippi as the environs of the West Jackson neighborhood where he lived with his mother and grandmother from the age of ten until he left in 1927. There was the physical desire and need for food, but there was also the hunger for books and knowledge that drove Wright to leave the South and eventually the United States and never return.

But even after Wright had quelled the physical hunger, he kept that feeling alive in his work. When he writes in *Black Boy* about his journey north, he speaks of it as "taking a part of the South to transplant in alien soil, to see if it could grow differently, if it could drink of new and cool rains, bend in strange winds, respond to the warmth of other suns, and, perhaps, to bloom." In those words, he is speaking of seeking nourishment and a means of quenching his thirst. The language is poetic, yet it is infused with the aesthetic of an art form shaped on his native soil, the blues. As Ralph Ellison notes in his 1945 essay "Richard Wright's Blues," "The blues is an impulse to keep the painful details and episodes of a brutal experience alive in one's aching consciousness, to finger its jagged grain, and to transcend it, not by the consolation of philosophy, but by squeezing from it a near-tragic, near-comic lyricism." In books such as *Uncle Tom's Children*, *Native Son*, *Black Boy*, *12 Million Black Voices*, and *The Outsider*, Wright reveals, whether consciously or unconsciously, how the hunger and blues he endured on the streets of West Jackson propelled his desire to write. The landscape of Mississippi may not be found very often on the pages of Richard Wright's writing, but the impact of his years on Mississippi soil are forever a part of his work.

Wright left Mississippi for Chicago in 1927 and lived there until 1937, working for the Federal Writers' Project his last two years in the Windy City. It was as a writer for this Depression-era program, which was part of the Works Progress Administration, that Wright met an aspiring author from New Orleans by the name of Margaret Walker. Along with several other writers, including Harlem Renaissance poet Arna Bontemps, Wright and Walker formed a writer's group on the South Side of Chicago. When Wright published his first book *Uncle Tom's Children* in 1938, his inscription in the copy he gave Walker read, "For Margaret, who if she only tries, will write a better book than this."

Margaret Walker and Richard Wright were equally ambitious, which made their relationship fraught and contentious. But Wright believed that Walker would become a published author. Walker's poetry collection *For My People* would win the Yale Younger Poets Prize, making her the first African American writer to secure that prize. After her time in Chicago, Walker eventually settled in Wright's hometown as a professor

Although they only became friends in the last twenty years of their lives, Eudora Welty and Margaret Walker shared an interest in literature and in leaving their literary legacy to the people of Mississippi.

at Jackson State University, not far from where Wright lived during his early years there.

In 1966, Walker would publish a novel, *Jubilee*, which traces the life of a slave woman, Vyry, whose story is based on Walker's great-grandmother. When asked how much of the novel is fact and how much is fiction, Walker said "the entire story follows a plot line of historical incidents from the first chapter until the last: the journeys, the Big Road, the violence, the battle" as well as documenting the places where her characters Vyry and Innis lived. The narrative ends in the 1960s on a train bound for Selma, Alabama, which connects the civil war with the civil rights movement.

Since its publication, *Jubilee* has never been out of print, but Walker's most tangible legacy is her founding of the Institute for the Study of the History, Life, and Culture of Black People at Jackson State University in 1968. It was one of the first centers for African American studies established in the country. Today that institute lives on as the Margaret Walker Center and is the home of Walker's personal papers. The center and the collection were built in the spirit of these lines from Walker's poem "For My People":

> For the cramped bewildered years we went to school to learn
> to know the reasons why and the answers to and the
> people who and the places where and the days when, in
> memory of the bitter hours when we discovered we
> were black and poor and small and different and nobody
> cared and nobody wondered and nobody understood;

Walker sought to break down the dividing line of inferiority that her friend Richard Wright once knew as being intimately part of Jackson.

WHEN KATHRYN STOCKETT WROTE her bestselling novel *The Help*, Eudora Welty's Belhaven neighborhood became part of the setting for a story of black maids working in white homes in 1960s Jackson. "Six days a week I take the bus across the Woodrow Wilson Bridge to where Miss Leefolt and all her white friends live in a place call Belhaven," the character Aibileen recalls. It is Jackson, Mississippi, just before the passage of the Civil Rights Act, and Aibileen notes how public transportation goes directly from black Jackson to white Jackson for the express purpose of ferrying black domestic help back and forth. The character Skeeter, a young white woman who decides to collect oral histories from black maids, asks Aibileen one day, "'Do you ever wish you could . . . change things?' [Skeeter] asks. And I can't help myself. I look at her head on. Cause that's one a the stupidest questions I ever heard. She got a confused, disgusted look on her face, like she done salted her coffee instead a sugared it. I turn back to my washing, so she don't see me rolling my eyes. 'Oh no, ma'am, everthing's fine.'"

A stretch of shops and restaurants in Jackson's Fondren district transformed to fit the time period of Kathryn Stockett's *The Help* during the filming of the movie.

While the maids and their relationship with their white employers is the focus of the narrative, *The Help* paints a picture of the lines of segregation and the inequities that have long been a part of Jackson. In the 1960s, while subdivisions were expanding in white neighborhoods, black Jacksonians were confined to a designated part of town. As Aibileen remarks early in the narrative, "As our numbers get bigger, we can't spread out. Our part a town just gets thicker."

In the same year in which *The Help* is set, Eudora Welty wrote "Where Is the Voice Coming From?" bravely capturing the feelings that were in the air in Jackson that year. Published in the *New Yorker*, "Where Is the Voice Coming From?" tells the story of the 1963 murder of civil rights activist Medgar Evers from the point of view of his assailant, Byron De La Beckwith. Welty wrote the story the same night that she learned of Evers's murder. When she heard the news, it occurred to her that she knew what was going on in the mind of the man who pulled the trigger. She knew because she had lived all of her life where it happened.

"It was the strangest feeling of horror and compulsion all in one," Welty commented in an interview almost ten years later. "I just meant by

A TALE OF TWO JACKSONS

the title that whoever was speaking, I—the writer—knew, was in a position to know, what the murderer must be saying and why."

Along with her *New Yorker* editor, William Maxwell, Welty edited the story many times. The result is a masterpiece of short fiction. Knowing a bit about the way Beckwith stalked Evers before gunning him down under his carport, I still get a chill every time I read these words:

> And there was his light on, waiting for me. In his garage, if you please. His car's gone. He's out planning still some other ways to do what we tell 'em they can't. I *thought* I'd beat him home. All I had to do was pick my tree and walk in close behind it.

The murder of Medgar Evers in 1963 forced Eudora Welty to confront the racism of her fellow white Mississippians. Welty believed that a novelist had a responsibility to bring alive both the mystery of humankind and the darkness. That's exactly what she does in this story: As you read the

Medgar Evers's house was designed without a front door—it could only be entered through the carport—to ensure the safety of his family.

closing line, you know she has captured life in Mississippi as it existed then, as well as the prevailing cultural mindset.

Margaret Walker's response to the murder of Medgar Evers, as a writer, was more personal because she and Evers lived on the same street in West Jackson. The effect Evers's murder had on the neighborhood was profound. Once the street had held a yearly Christmas celebration with lights and a pageant. There was even an active garden club in the neighborhood. That changed after the Evers assassination. After the Evers murder, the street was dark at Christmas. Walker wrote two poems about Evers: "Micha," which characterizes Micha/Medgar as a prophet and the sonnet "Medgar Evers, 1925–1963: Arlington Cemetery":

> The birds overhead will build their nests;
> In the twilight hours sing a serenade.
> The grass will gradually creep into shade
> Where this martyred man sleeps unafraid.
> And he will have neighbors good and true
> Who have given their lives for freedom, too.

Margaret Walker connected the freedom struggle of the civil rights era with an ancient prophetic voice, one that she wanted to keep alive. It was this desire, her work with Richard Wright during the Chicago Black Renaissance, and her later work with the leaders of the Black Arts Movement that inspired Walker to leave behind the archive in Jackson that now bears her name. By creating an archive of the work of black writers, Walker hoped to inspire the next generation and connect them with the past. "The body of my work," she wrote, "springs from my interest in a historical point of view that is central to the development of black people as we approach the twenty-first century." Novelists Kiese Laymon and Angie Thomas are part of the black people, black writers, of the twenty-first century Margaret Walker had in mind.

Kiese Laymon practically grew up on the campus of Jackson State University, where his mother taught political science. His mother saw Margaret Walker, who taught at Jackson State for thirty years, as a mentor. So Laymon essentially came of age in the shadow of Margaret Walker's archive, having visited her home as a young man. Laymon remembers Walker's house as the only place in Jackson with more books, folders, and African masks than his own house. On one visit Walker even presented Laymon with a copy of Nikki Giovanni's *Cotton Candy on a Rainy Day*, after admonishing him to "own" his name. After reading Giovanni and then Walker's "For My People," Laymon was confused by this stanza from her poem: "Let a race of men now rise and take control." Laymon told me, "I didn't understand what a 'race of men' looked like, or why Margaret Walker ended the poem hoping a group of men would rise and take control."

From a young age, the way Laymon saw himself as a writer was rooted in a different South than the one that had shaped and influenced Walker. "I try hard as I can to never 'represent' the South," Laymon told writer Roxane Gay in 2013, after the release of his novel *Long Division* and his essay collection *How to Slowly Kill Yourself and Others in America*. "I want to explore my South, honor my South, extend the traditions of my South, but I don't want to represent it, translate it, or synthesize it for folks unwilling to love or imagine our people. The South, generally, and Mississippi, specifically, is home. It's home. It's why I read, why I write, why I try to love, and why it's hard as hell to beat me. We have been and can be a model of transformation for the rest of the nation and world. But we gotta stop being so devoted to death and destruction."

Walker saw her collection as a means of preserving the past, while Laymon sees his writing as a way of reckoning with and acknowledging the past without feeling weighted down by it. History is something to be understood, rather than a burden to carry. The raw honesty of Laymon's writing honors Walker's ideas about blackness and the South while at the same time critiquing and questioning certain assumptions from the past. The Mississippi that Laymon writes about is informed by someone whose life, unlike Walker's, was not defined in terms of black uplift.

What Laymon sees on Mississippi's landscape is what I would characterize as "post-integration blues." These are different from the traditional sense of the blues, as found in the work of Richard Wright. Post-integration blues are a meditation on the power dynamic that exists while growing up black in Mississippi in the post–civil rights era. Laymon's post-integration blues layers his narratives with a personal perspective that acknowledges the continuing existence of white supremacy. At the same time, he allows his own ideas of truth, possibility, and blackness to shine through without being defined or constrained by the forces of white supremacy. Wright's blues projected a powerlessness against white domination in the South, while Laymon feels compelled to assert his power to fight against it. In spite of the existence of the blues that Laymon says exist under what he calls "central Mississippi skies," he sees beauty in this mélange of hurt and joy, rain and sunshine, but nothing with a perfect, uncomplicated storybook ending. Unlike Wright, Laymon sees no reason to leave or escape Mississippi. It is a place where he feels safe and at home. Life is messy, and so is life in Mississippi, so why not stay? "I know that I've been slowly killed by folks who were as feverishly in need of life and death as I am. The really confusing part is that a few of those folks who have nudged me closer to slow death have also helped me say yes to life when I most needed it."

One of the places that Laymon felt slowly killed him was across town from Jackson State at Millsaps College, where he was expelled for taking a copy of *The Red Badge of Courage* out of the library without properly checking it out. But it was also at Millsaps where he discovered Toni Cade Bambara, a writer who was part of Margaret Walker's circle. It's something Laymon recounts in his memoir *Heavy*:

115

Bambara took what [Eudora] Welty did best and created worlds where no one was sheltered, cloistered, or white, but everyone . . . was weird, wonderful, slightly wack, and all the way black. . . . Writing required something more than just practice, something more than reading, too. It required loads of unsentimental explorations of black love. It required an acceptance of our strange. And mostly, it required a commitment to new structures, not reformation.

Kiese Laymon is a Mississippi writer who has committed himself to looking for new structures for writing about his native land, free of sentimental Southern tropes and the burden of Southern history. Laymon's Mississippi is gritty and dirty, with real beauty underneath the shroud of dust and shadows from the past that he acknowledges exist yet by which he does not allow himself to be defined.

Angie Thomas's novels for young adults are written with a similar sensibility, one that is rooted in the post-integration blues of the present but not overshadowed by the past. Thomas has said that she did not want to set her work in a specific city or state in order to allow her readers to imagine themselves in the setting. And while her novels *The Hate U Give* and *On the Come Up* are not set in Mississippi, the neighborhood Garden Heights is inspired by the Georgetown neighborhood of Jackson where Thomas grew up. In using the Georgetown neighborhood as inspiration, Thomas reveals how the

Vacant commercial buildings in downtown Jackson.

landscape of Mississippi can be used by a writer to create something that is universal rather than regional. "There's a lot of good in my neighborhood, but there's bad, too," Thomas recalled in a talk she gave to a group of booksellers in 2018. She knows firsthand about the bad that existed in

Under central Mississippi skies like these, Jackson-born writer Kiese Laymon sees both beauty and pain.

her neighborhood, having been caught in the cross fire of a shoot-out there when she was six years old.

After I read Thomas's work I decided to visit her old neighborhood just to see the landscape that inspired it. While Thomas thinks of the Jackson neighborhood where she grew up as a place where no one goes, I know that has not always been the case. That spring afternoon I had not anticipated confronting my own memories of playing in that same area. Thomas's hometown neighborhood is just blocks away from Margaret Walker Alexander Drive, which is where Margaret Walker once lived and where she asked Kiese Laymon to "own his name." When I visited Margaret Walker's street as a young boy, it was called Guynes Street. It was a neighborhood of one-story ranch houses perched atop lush green lawns and occupied by black professionals like my friend's father, who was a pharmacist and operated a drugstore on Farish Street, Jackson's black business district. For black Jackson at the time, Thomas's old neighborhood was the place to be rather than one to be avoided. It was a place where I always felt safe, yet as I walked that street as a boy no one spoke of or acknowledged the tragedy that had visited one house on the block, the murder of Medgar Evers. Evers's house could be seen from my friend's front yard. I had walked by numerous times and never knew that the house on Guynes Street was once occupied by Evers and his family.

To understand Mississippi, you must probe the silences, because it is in the things people are reluctant to discuss that the truth lies. Finding the truth in Mississippi is something Jackson-based investigative reporter Jerry Mitchell knows intimately, since he has spent a career opening up things in Mississippi's past that have been covered up by reticence, shame, and malice. Always curious about why Evers's murderer, Byron De La Beckwith, was never convicted, Mitchell learned from research in the archives of the Mississippi State Sovereignty Commission that at the same time that the State of Mississippi was prosecuting Beckwith, the Sovereignty Commission—which was headed by the governor—was secretly assisting the defense in trying to get him acquitted. They even tampered with the selection of the jury. Mitchell's reporting led to the eventual conviction of Beckwith in 1994, a story that he recalls in his book on civil rights–era cold cases, *Race Against Time*. What Mitchell did was open up the story in a way that let Medgar Evers's former neighbors know they no longer had to restrain themselves from reckoning with the past.

Silence about the violent past on Guynes Street served as a means of not instilling fear in the children who grew up in the neighborhood or, for those like me, who visited. But that same silence also served as a means of masking the truth of what happened there. That afternoon when I visited the Medgar Evers Home Museum—a house that Evers directed to have built without a front door specifically for his family's safety—I had expected to encounter Angie Thomas's world but instead collided with my own past and how it can sometimes be caught between memory and forgetting.

But that is what Mississippi is like. In the silences we create under central Mississippi skies, we also find how we are connected. Eudora Welty and Margaret Walker, while contemporaries, only came to know each other in the last twenty years of their lives. Both writers chose to leave their archives in Mississippi and to preserve the places they loved—Welty's Belhaven home and Walker's Jackson State—in the Magnolia State's literary landscape. Angie Thomas and Kiese Laymon are writers who look at the world with a connection to a past we all share, though from a perspective that is free of the historical burdens about the civil rights era to which my generation clasps tightly. Theirs may be a post–integration era blues, but there is more that connects us than separates us. Our blues are more united than they are divided.

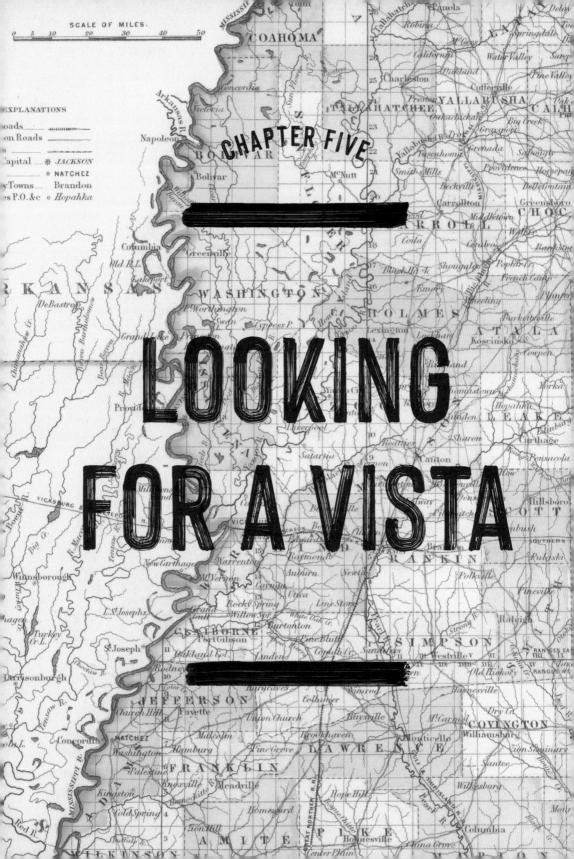

CHAPTER FIVE

LOOKING
FOR A VISTA

In Mississippi it is difficult to achieve a vista.

—Barry Hannah, "Testimony of Pilot"

"*SITTING BY THE POOL* at six o'clock I felt the euphoria of Interstate America," Joan Didion wrote in her notebook during a visit to Meridian, Mississippi, in 1970. Didion soon learned from a gregarious local radio station owner dressed in a bright green shirt that Meridian sat in the heart of Mississippi's eastern hills near the Mississippi Alabama border. She also learned that pulpwood was the heart of the local economy. "This man in the green shirt had laid Meridian out before us as an entrepreneur's dream," Didion remarked in her notebook after hearing the man's vision for the myriad national franchises that should line the town's streets and intersections. In the dining room of Weidmann's—a Meridian institution and the oldest restaurant in Mississippi—Joan Didion gained a fuller sense of the town and began to see it as more than just a spot to speed past along the interstate.

The Howard Johnson's and the pool that Didion believed could have been anywhere in America are now gone, having made way for other national businesses the man in the green shirt predicted would soon become a part of Meridian. Meridian is a town that in a sense has always been a crossroads of sorts, having been established in 1860 at the junction of the Mobile and Ohio Railroad and the Southern Railroad. Burned by General William Tecumseh Sherman in the battle of Meridian during the Civil War, the town was rebuilt and reimagined. Jimmie Rodgers, the singing brakeman often described as the father of country music, grew up in Meridian during this period of change and transition. His travels on the railroads that intersected this then-booming east Mississippi town helped spread his music across the South. The pattern of the reimagined Meridian is one Rodgers would recognize even today, a layout sometimes described as a spiderweb of streets intersecting at various angles. In the middle of them all is a commanding seventeen-story Art Deco skyscraper called the Threefoot Building. It dwarfs the smaller buildings around it, dominating the streetscape and capturing the imagination of those who encounter it.

Given the way Meridian has rebuilt and reinvented itself, it is fitting that novelist Brad Watson reimagined his hometown as a setting for his fiction. The town of Mercury in his novels *The Heaven of Mercury* and *Miss Jane*, as well as in various pieces of short fiction in his collections *Last Days of the Dog-Men* and *Aliens in the Prime of Their Lives*, in many ways serves as a doppelgänger for Meridian. In Watson's fiction, the Threefoot Building becomes the Dreyfus Building, "at fifteen stories the closest thing to a sky-scraper Mercury had. From a great distance it appeared to stand like a lone building left after a cyclone, though actually surrounded by . . . smaller buildings in this slowly dying downtown." Watson describes Mercury as in a valley that "was a river basin once thicketed with tall pines and broadleaf and run by bear, panther, deer, raccoon, bobcat, coyote, and flown by all manner of birds." But Watson is careful to note that Mercury and Meridian are separate and distinct places, given the liberties he has taken in his fiction with regard to geographical, historical, and demographic facts.

In *The Heaven of Mercury* Watson recasts and reshapes Meridian's most memorable places: Weidmann's becomes Schoenhof's, and he throws in the real names of buildings such as the Temple Theater. His story "Aliens in the Prime of Their Lives" takes place in the haunting, old Gothic main building and grounds of East Mississippi State Hospital, which began its life as Mississippi Hospital for the Insane.

Downtown Meridian, with the Threefoot Building, was reimagined by Brad Watson as the fictional town of Mercury.

Weidmann's, Mississippi's oldest restaurant, was reimagined as
Schoenhof's in Brad Watson's *The Heaven of Mercury*.

Had Didion headed north rather than east when she left Meridian, she
would have encountered the Appalachian foothills, which in some of the
surrounding cattle farms in the green of the spring and early summer can
feel more English than Southern. Now much of this land has been planted
in pine forest, something Watson noticed when he returned to create the
setting for his novel *Miss Jane*. "I did return to Meridian several times while
I was writing *Miss Jane*. I didn't need to return to downtown so much as I
needed to visit the land where my mother, and before her my great aunt
Mary Ellis 'Jane' Clay, grew up on small farms across the dirt road from
one another."

"The farm land is now pine tree land, and has been for a couple of
generations," Watson learned when he returned. "But there were ruins
of the dogtrot my mother grew up in, which burned in a fire when I was
a child. The pine forest is now dense, but the old sandy road still winds

through it, and I found remains of the farming operation in the woods above the old creek that still trickles through there. I wanted to revisit the feel of the land, the air, smells, birdsong. My mother had told me, years ago, what the place used to look like before it effectively became woods again. I could stand there, see the topography through the trees, imagine what this field, that pasture looked like when they farmed it. Where the cattle pond was, the house, the outbuildings. She told me about those things, and some of them I probably just imagined." As he wrote from his home in Wyoming, Watson realized the line between what really was and what was imagined had begun to blur.

Miss Jane was inspired by the true story of Watson's own great aunt, who was born just outside of Meridian in the early twentieth century. While it is a novel more about the body—particularly a genital birth defect that renders Jane incontinent—Watson uses place and setting to allow the reader to connect with his central character, a relative he never knew but heard so much about. Jane is adopted by a country doctor who seeks to find a treatment for her condition and Watson felt he needed to find and define a space for where these two characters would interact. "The doctor's woods in *Miss Jane* comes from a section of virgin forest that bordered my little dead-end street when I was growing up, and we used to wander in there all the time. Those woods may be the most fertile place for me in terms of generating sense of place in memories of Meridian as well as the creation of Mercury, followed of course by those downtown spots."

It is those memories that situate his characters in a particular place and time. In *Miss Jane*, Watson describes the world that his character Jane came into, writing, "She was born into that time and place, in the farmland cut from the pine and broadleaf woods of east-central Mississippi, 1915, when there was no possibility of doing anything to alleviate her condition, no medical procedure to correct it. It was something to be accepted,

Farmland outside of Meridian, the setting of Brad Watson's *Miss Jane*.

grim-faced, as they accepted crop failure, debt, poverty, the frequent death of infants and small children from fevers and other maladies."

Barry Hannah may have believed that in Mississippi it is hard to achieve a vista, but the hills of northeast Mississippi north of Meridian are the closest thing to it. The hills, often spread out between small valleys, stretch out long and wide in this part of the state before they get smaller and more irregular the farther north you go. It is Mississippi's idea of a vista, one that Philadelphia, Mississippi, writer and photographer Florence Mars began to take note of with her pen and Graflex camera after moving back to her native Neshoba County from New Orleans in the 1950s. "In Neshoba

Given the sometimes flat and hilly terrain, it is difficult to achieve a vista in east Mississippi.

CHAPTER FIVE

County, Mississippi, the basement of the past is not very deep," Mars wrote in her memoir *Witness in Philadelphia*. "All mysteries of the present seem to be entangled in the total history of the county, a history that began in 1830." In 1830 the Choctaw Indians ceded land around Neshoba County, the last of their lands east of the Mississippi River, in the Treaty of Dancing Rabbit Creek. The families that came to the region from the Carolinas and Georgia then remade the landscape through cotton farming. By the time Mars returned to Philadelphia, Mississippi, in 1954, another change to the landscape was afoot. The Brown v. Board of Education decision on school integration had white Mississippians up in arms, worried that the racial geography of the state would be transformed by school integration, voting rights, and civil rights. "Because I knew the street scenes of Philadelphia would soon begin to change, I bought a camera and an enlarger, built a darkroom, and began to snap thousands of pictures."

Florence Mars's writing and photography provide an example of how the relationship between what we see and what we know is never settled. When Mars began to photograph Philadelphia and the rest of Neshoba County, she thought she was merely capturing a period of waning agrarian innocence as well as the remnants of a segregated society, one that would soon change or fade away. But in 1964 the relationship between what she captured with the lens of her camera and what she experienced and knew about her community also began to change. In June 1964 three civil rights workers—Michael Schwerner, James Chaney, and Andrew Goodman—disappeared after investigating the burning of a church in the nearby Mt. Zion Baptist Church community. Local newspapers, including the *Meridian Star*, suggested that the disappearance was a hoax and publicity stunt on the part of the civil rights workers. After the bodies of the young men were pulled from an earthen dam, Mars began to realize the extent of the involvement of the Ku Klux Klan in the murders. "I knew the majority of the community saw the killings in racial terms: the COFO [a civil rights

The burned-out Ford station wagon driven by slain civil rights workers Michael Schwerner, James Chaney, and Andrew Goodman after it was found in the Bogue Chitto swamp, some thirteen miles northeast of Philadelphia, Mississippi.

group] workers were the enemy and whatever happened to them was justified and deserved," Mars wrote. "However, I knew I would do what I could not only to assist the FBI but, if it was in my power, to help the civil leadership see the issue and act."

Witness in Philadelphia is Mars's story of how the way she saw her hometown changed, as well as the actions she took in the wake of the Freedom Summer murders in 1964. It is a book Mars struggled to write. When Mars looked at her community she did not like what she saw, yet her history with the people and the land made it difficult for her to distance herself from the place. When it was published in 1977, Mars credited her collaborator, Gail Falk, with helping her "to assimilate the material" about her hometown. What Falk did was help Mars connect what she saw with what she knew of a place that was changing and continuing to change.

DRIVING NORTH FROM PHILADELPHIA, Mississippi, the hills become smaller and the valleys between them wider. In the east Mississippi Hills the terrain shifts on the trip from south to north; the northernmost hills are really the foothills of the Appalachians, which change in size and range the farther south you travel. Sometimes the hills are small rises on the horizon, sometimes they are larger. With the constantly changing scale of the landscape in this region comes varying perspectives on how writers choose to describe the place or choose not to engage with it. Tennessee Williams may have been born in the town of Columbus, on its gentle hills bordering the Tombigbee River, yet the literary canvas he chose was the Delta and New Orleans. Novelist Catherine Lacey's family may own the hardware store in Tupelo where Elvis Presley bought his first guitar, yet in spite of a connection to a place that is a virtual cultural reliquary for one of the region's secular saints, she feels little that ties her to the land that shaped her. "I do not love the place I am obliged to call home," Lacey wrote in an essay for *The Believer*. "I love some people who live in Mississippi. I

The landscape begins to level out on the drive north from Philadelphia.

love the kudzu, ponds, and live oaks; I am fond of opossums, will drink a julep, have enjoyed a biscuit or two, but I do not love this place generally, and I detest the way the past—buttressed by political and social inequalities—cleaves to the present."

Journalist Ida B. Wells left her hometown of Holly Springs, Mississippi, for Memphis, but her anti-lynching activism eventually drove her away from the South to Chicago. Her desire to expose the injustice that plagued Mississippi and the South placed her in intense personal danger. Memphis may have been a city her fellow Mississippian Richard Wright found more hospitable than his hometown of Jackson, but Wells—and eventually Wright—found this liminal space between North and South as dangerous as the Hill Country that touches the Tennessee state line. Wells advised black people to leave Memphis because "neither character nor standing avails the Negro if he dares to protect himself against the white man or become his rival."

Whether one stays or leaves this part of Mississippi—or any region of the state for that matter—the urge to explain it and understand it never leaves your consciousness. Perhaps that is why the hills around William Dunlap's native Webster County serve as both literary and artistic inspiration for him. The stories he gathered in his collection *Short Mean Fiction* had their origin in his hybrid artist sketchbook and journal. Dunlap says that "hypothetical realism" guides his sketches, stories, and paintings. "The places and things I paint and describe are not real, but they could be," he says of his work. As for his fiction, "none of what I have written really happened, but it could have."

Yet a drive through Webster County and the land around his hometown of Mathiston sometimes feels as if you have entered one of Dunlap's paintings. You'll encounter the occasional abandoned cotton gin or barn on the horizon as well as a field of rolling hills filled with haybales. Yet, rather than merely capturing the pastoral nature of the remnants of the agrarian South, Dunlap injects visual commentary into his painting, just as he does into his fiction. One painting that tells the story of this landscape is "Meditations on the Origins of Agriculture in America."

Amid a landscape inspired by his native county, two visual elements in the painting stand out: a man's body pierced by numerous arrows (a reference to an image of Saint Sebastian) and a Confederate flag. The flag's presence speaks to the presence of slavery in Mississippi. It is impossible to think of the origins of agriculture in Mississippi and America without coming to grips with the symbol of the Confederate flag; it is impossible to see the Confederate flag and not think of its connection to the institution of slavery as well as the white supremacy that influenced events in these hills well after the end of the Civil War. Of equal historical importance to Dunlap's painting is the forcible removal

William Dunlap's "Meditations on the Origins of Agriculture in America" serves as a reminder that the one constant in art and life is the land.

of the American Indians, signified by the body pierced with arrows. "The 1830s Treaty of Dancing Rabbit Creek opened the rich bottomlands of north central Mississippi to my ancestors who came here and stayed," Dunlap notes, and he recognizes that the land he owns on this landscape belonged to the native Choctaw people who had occupied it for centuries before they were removed. "The handmade rake, the piece of firewood with the pulley grown over, the drips and splatters, the snakeskin are all significant in their own way and they come together inside the frame to speak honestly about the origins of agriculture in America," Dunlap noted when this painting was donated to the University of Mississippi Museum. "This is something I would hope we remember and meditate on from time to time."

Even in a state with abundant farms and farmland, few contemporary Mississippi writers focus on the relationship between the land and those who till its soil. Although the setting lies to the west of Webster County, Jamie Kornegay's *Soil* is one of the few contemporary books from a Mississippi writer that has a farmer as a protagonist. But Kornegay's character Jay Mize, an organic farmer in the Mississippi Hills bordering the Delta, is not living a bucolic rural life that allows him to meditate on the origins of Mississippi agriculture. *Soil* is a gothic story of Jay's descent into paranoid delusion, which destroys most of his personal relationships. In a state where fewer and fewer farms are owned by actual farmers, people like Jay Mize are rare. Today it is more common for farms to be owned by investors in boardrooms and to be industrial operations. An agrarian lifestyle in contemporary Mississippi is more of an idea than an actuality.

Near the setting of Kornegay's *Soil*, on the edge of the Mississippi Hills, at the end of twists and turns in the road, sits the town of Water Valley. Once a railway hub and a business center for the surrounding agricultural community, in the twenty-first century the town has reinvented itself as a

Violet Valley Bookstore in Water Valley makes queer, feminist, and multicultural books available in this small community and is the only LGBTQ bookstore in the state.

community for artists. An old drugstore is now an art gallery, which is just down the street from the Violet Valley Bookstore, a bookstore driven by the mission to make feminist, queer, and multicultural books available to local citizens.

The existence of a place like Violet Valley Bookstore would have been unimaginable to Hubert Creekmore, a novelist, poet, editor, and translator who was born in this town in 1907. Creekmore was an openly gay man in New York in the 1940s and 1950s—as open as one could be in those days—yet when he visited Mississippi and Water Valley he could only be thought of under the seemingly benign label "confirmed bachelor." In his hometown today, he would not feel the urgent need to hide his identity.

Although his family moved to Jackson when he was a young man, he attended the University of Mississippi just up the road from Water Valley, which made it easy for him to return to his hometown. In early adulthood this proximity to Water Valley allowed Creekmore to take a close look at the town that had shaped his childhood memories. While in Jackson his family lived on the same street as Eudora Welty—eventually his sister married Welty's brother—and Welty and Creekmore served as early readers of each other's writing. Yet Water Valley rather than Jackson became Creekmore's literary touchstone. His poem "To the Very Late Mourners of the Old South" reads like a meditation on what his hometown had become in the 1940s when it was just another small town in Hill Country rather than one bustling with trains and farmers on a Saturday morning:

> Come—decay has crushed your crinolines,
> forgetfulness has rusted over the graces
> of your courtesy. Too long your faces
> now have poured their maudlin might-have-beens

in tears upon the fond remembered scenes

that make the artificial wreath time places

on your tomb of adolescence.

In addition to his poetry, Hubert Creekmore was the author of three novels, all set in the town of Ashton, a fictionalized version of Water Valley: both places have "no courthouse square," a typical feature in small towns in this part of Mississippi. "The stores, cafes, hotels, and garages were aligned on the town's main highway, which crossed and re-crossed on wide bridges the stream that drained the valley." Walking down the street in Water Valley today, you can see how Creekmore captured his hometown in unmistakable detail. Just over a decade ago, when many of the storefronts were empty, it would have been harder to match the fictional place with the real one. Now that this town is being revived, the descriptions from Creekmore's fiction become recognizable.

The childhood home of writer Hubert Creekmore in Water Valley.

In his social realist fiction, Creekmore tackles religion, race, and sexuality in a way that, at the time, set him apart as a Mississippi writer, particularly one from a prominent family. Published in 1946, his first novel, *The Fingers of the Night*, confronts religious fanaticism in Mississippi and how it affects the life of his character Tessie Andrews. The *Jackson Daily News* described *The Fingers of the Night* as belonging in the garbage can with *Sanctuary*, *Light in August*, *Tobacco Road*, and "any other nasty drivel purporting to picture life in Mississippi." *The Chain in the Heart*, his second book, confronted the issue of race and Jim Crow in the South and probably would have earned Creekmore a similarly scathing review in Mississippi, particularly since the black-owned *Jet* magazine named it in their "Book of the Week" column on August 6, 1953. They even published a photo of "Mississippi-born Creekmore." The reviewer wrote, "*The Chain in the Heart* is one thought-provoking message which spells out clearly the implications of freedom. The message: that although a man is 'free,' he may still wear fetters; that it is of little use to emancipate the body if the mind and the heart are to remain chained to the past."

But it is his third novel, *The Welcome*, that has brought contemporary interest in the work of Hubert Creekmore and scholars of the queer South now view it as an underground classic. His protagonist Don Mason returns to his hometown of Ashton, Mississippi, after living in New York. With Don's return, he and his friend Jim Furlow are forced to confront their feelings for each other and their mutual sexual attraction. However, Jim's marriage and small-town expectations continue to cast a shadow over their feelings. In a disappointed and disingenuous gesture, Jim even advises Don to get married; it is, as he says in a voice tinged with irony, "a fine thing—the only way to be happy," but when Don reluctantly admits that he might marry their mutual friend Isabel, Jim's "face grew sad and his eyes filled with a solemn, helpless yearning."

There is nothing sexually explicit in *The Welcome*, and the desire Jim and Don have for each other is coded rather than direct, which may or may not have been an editorial decision. "Creekmore wasn't happy with how *The Welcome* was handled editorially," filmmaker Mary Stanton Knight recalled, based on the research for her short documentary on Creekmore, "Dear Hubert." *The Welcome* is dedicated to Ted Rearick, Creekmore's editor who left the publishing house before *The Welcome* was released.

Hubert Creekmore died in a taxi in New York in 1967, suffering a heart attack on the way to the airport for a trip to Spain. For some time after his death his luggage remained at the airport terminal and his apartment in New York remained locked and unvisited. Had he lived longer, perhaps there would have been answers to the questions his work seems to bring up about his relationship with his hometown, with Mississippi, and with the social circle that shaped him. As Creekmore wrote in *The Welcome*, "Did anyone else in Ashton ever dream of something beyond, something richer in life—not the fake richness of religion—something that would enrich their world, small as it was, and make sense of their efforts to earn money?" Hubert Creekmore did dream of a world beyond his hometown, which may be why he felt the need to return to it again and again in his fiction. Perhaps by creating a fictional analogue to his hometown, Creekmore was able to achieve some measure of distance, both for the sake of the creative process and for the pushback that often came from people unhappy with his portrayal of Mississippi.

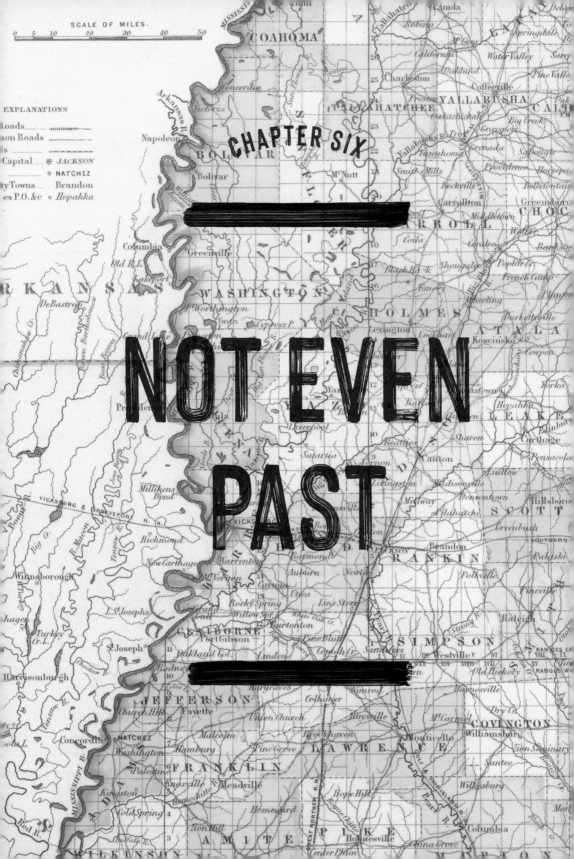

CHAPTER SIX

NOT EVEN PAST

Don't you see? This whole land, the whole South, is cursed, and all of us who derive from it, whom it ever suckled, white and black both, lie under the curse?

—William Faulkner, *Go Down, Moses*

William Faulkner's Rowan Oak lies at the end of a wooded street in Oxford, Mississippi. It is hard to look at its white columns without thinking of the way memory casts a shadow on the landscape of the town Faulkner called home.

*F*EW RESIDENTS OF WATER VALLEY are aware of how their little town has been memorialized in Hubert Creekmore's three works of fiction, in spite of the prominent historical marker that sits in front of the white Victorian house where Creekmore grew up with his family. In Mississippi's fictional geography, Ashton and its county have been overshadowed by Faulkner's Yoknapatawpha and his imaginary municipality of Jefferson, which is represented by the town of Oxford just twenty miles up the road from Water Valley. Unlike Water Valley, Oxford has a courthouse square that serves as the center of the community.

The fourteen novels William Faulkner set in Yoknapatawpha, from *Sartoris* in 1929 to *The Reivers* in 1962, have made it the most famous county in American literature. Because of the writers who are devoted to the settings that shaped and inspired them, Mississippi literary landscape has a pied beauty, with all of its diverse and varied settings from the Gulf Coast to Hill Country. But for many, the only place that fits in the imagination of what Mississippi and the South is like is the world William Faulkner created. And even that is a setting that is changing and evolving even as much remains the same.

If Mississippi lives in the American imagination as the South writ large, the town of Oxford serves as the literary home of the mythic South. It was a creative leap in the imagination of Nobel Laureate William Faulkner that elevated the place he called his "postage stamp of native soil" into this

A view of the Oxford square, a site of William Faulkner's frequent walks.

heightened realm and in turn interwove a real place into an imagined one. Walking through Oxford you can see how this town could spark the imagination, both in the past and today. The occasional Greek Revival mansion brings to mind the romantic idea of the old South while the tidy bungalow across the street from the mansion serves as a reminder that the realities of the new South began to overtake the mythologized one more than half a century ago. But underneath the formalist visage of Oxford, the bohemian bubbles up alongside the traditional.

Oxford has long been a town where artists and thinkers coexisted alongside farmers and tradesmen, albeit with some tension. William Faulkner's artistic ambitions were dismissed by the locals who named him "Count, No 'Count," since making art was not considered real work. Even after his work drew international acclaim, to the people of Oxford

CHAPTER SIX

A muscadine arbor beside the barn at William Faulkner's Rowan Oak.

Faulkner was still nothing more than a foppish, pretentious dandy. But the creative community of writers and artists that has grown here since his death seems like Faulkner's revenge against those who once scorned him. Jackson may be the state capital, but Oxford has become the center of the state's literary culture.

The transformation of Oxford began when Faulkner overlaid the geography of Oxford in Lafayette County with his imagined town of Jefferson in Yoknapatawpha County. Both places rest on the edge of the Black Prairie of the Mississippi Hills, a region of the state where Appalachia meets the Deep South. Like Lafayette County, Yoknapatawpha County has the Tallahatchie River in the north. In the southern part he renames the Yocona River of Lafayette County as the Yoknapatawpha River, the older Native American name for the Yocona. With this changing of names layered over actual places, you see how Faulkner's world blends the real with the imagined. With the shifting of objects, places, and events around the Mississippi Hills region, he creates a unique topography of place while at the same time describing the universal experiences of humankind. The land and its people were the source for his artistic creations, but the day-to-day work of writing took place at his Greek Revival home called Rowan Oak.

At the end of a wooded street in Oxford, Faulkner's Rowan Oak remains frozen in time, his beloved home standing as a living embodiment of the words he wrote in the pages of *Light in August*: "memory believes before knowing remembers." You can even get a sense of Faulkner's creative process on the walls of his study, where he sketched out chapters for his novel *A Fable* in graphite and red grease pencil. Since it is now a museum, everything inside is as Faulkner left it upon his death, right down to the 1962 directory that sits beside the phone where Faulkner received news of his Nobel Prize in Literature in 1949.

It's hard to look at the white columns of Rowan Oak without thinking of the way memory casts its shadow on the landscape of this little town, because Faulkner believed that memory loomed over the past and

William Faulkner's study, where he sketched out chapters for his novel *A Fable* on the walls.

influenced the present and the future. Sometimes it seems as if this house, frozen in time, is holding the past safely in place and allowing time to click by with little intrusion from the present. But Rowan Oak is not just a place that holds Faulkner's past.

When Faulkner purchased Rowan Oak in 1930, he purchased a property with direct links to slavery and the story of the University of Mississippi. Robert Sheegog, the original owner of Rowan Oak, was an early settler in Oxford, Mississippi, as well as a merchant, cotton producer, and slave owner. Payment records from the 1840s in the archives of the University of Mississippi indicate that Sheegog, along with other local slave owners, also loaned slaves to the university. The university records characterized the use of slaves as "servant hires." These servant hires would have labored to build the university, which was founded in 1848.

It is difficult to say whether Faulkner gained any literary inspiration from his knowledge that slaves once housed on the grounds of the home he later occupied helped construct the University of Mississippi. Possibly not, as the slave dwelling on the grounds of Rowan Oak was only designated as

Rowan Oak has direct ties to the history of slavery in Oxford. Although William Faulkner used it as a smokehouse, this building was once a slave dwelling.

NOT EVEN PAST

such after research led by historians and anthropologists at the University of Mississippi in recent years. However, the institution of slavery plays a significant role in his 1936 masterpiece *Absalom, Abasalom!*, which also has the University of Mississippi as a backdrop. Whether Faulkner's writing was influenced by the link between his home and slavery is something we may never know, but we do know that Faulkner's novels emphasized the presence of the past, as well as the value of endurance. *Absalom, Absalom!* is a novel about how the past lingers and how that past, when not confronted constructively, can be destructive. It is an interesting coincidence that Faulkner was only able to grapple with the issue of slavery in his fiction after he purchased Rowan Oak and was surrounded by remnants of the peculiar institution.

OUTSIDE OF THE GROUNDS of Rowan Oak, the Oxford Faulkner knew rarely intrudes on a visitor's consciousness. Yes, the courthouse still looms over the Square in Oxford, giving you a flavor of the fictional Jefferson, where life was lived with that Faulknerian triumvirate of grief, fury, and despair. But what else of Faulkner's world remains on the landscape of Oxford? Without a doubt the Square has lost the grittiness of Faulkner's time, with few signs of the farms and farmers that once lay outside Oxford's city limits. The Square's gleaming shops are the living embodiment of his character Flem Snopes's unbridled ambition, though it's difficult to imagine that crude and contemptible member of the Snopes clan walking through the doors of any of them, much less ambling along the Square's streets. That's why the search for Faulkner's world begins at Rowan Oak, because that is the place where Faulkner constructed his imaginary Yoknapatawpha. Given all the change to Oxford's landscape since his death, Faulkner's world can sometimes be difficult to imagine today outside Rowan Oak's boundaries.

Faulkner's genius lies in how his fiction captured the error and anguish of the American South with poetic reality while at the same time uncovering something universal and profound. Readers of Faulkner come to Oxford because they know the place holds the essence of what he wrote about and to pay homage to the landscape that fed his imagination. For Faulkner, a sense of place was an attitude assumed while doing something else on the page. What Faulkner did by exploring place was to dig deep into the vagaries of the human condition.

To truly appreciate the place that inspired Faulkner, you must read his work, which I admit looms as a mountain too high to climb for many readers, with his long, complex sentences and shifting point of view. The key to reading Faulkner is to realize that, like any writer, an essential part of his toolkit in constructing a narrative is to withhold and gradually reveal information. The joy of reading Faulkner is just to let go of the linear way we look at the world and time and realize that his narrative is often an expression of the interior life of his characters. In *Absalom, Absalom!* Faulkner slowly unspools the story of Thomas Sutpen and his family to keep the reader engaged with this complex allegory of the South and to build tension in the novel's nonlinear narrative. To enjoy Faulkner, a reader must enter the world he created and just go along for the ride.

When I am reading Faulkner, his novels and stories take me back to a different time, a time before I was born. By contrasting the Mississippi of my youth and the one that exists today with the world Faulkner knew, I feel part of a continuum, one that is connected not just to the Mississippi of my birth but to the wider world Faulkner was trying to reach. That feeling is even stronger when I am in the land that inspired Faulkner and attempt to look at the place through his lens. He had a defining eye, but a subversive one as well, and he looked at things others chose not to look at or to avoid. By being subversive, Faulkner enlarged the vision of the world he came from. Perhaps he knew that the place he wrote about would eventually change or be transformed, so his fiction serves to keep his Oxford frozen in time while still speaking to the universality of the human condition.

In the years since Faulkner walked the streets of Oxford, the world he once knew has been refashioned beyond what he could have ever imagined. The Big Woods, the wide swath of wild, open land that was the setting of many of Faulkner's Yoknapatawpha stories, has faded from view, replaced by subdivisions and luxury estates. The field that provided Faulkner's setting for McCaslin's field in *The Sound and the Fury* is now a golf course. On the Oxford Square the new South dominates the old South—with a white marble Confederate statue being the last holdout from the past, albeit an imagined past. Yet the essence of the place Faulkner wrote about remains on this landscape. There is even a sculpture of Faulkner himself sitting on a bench on the edge of Courthouse Square. With or without the statue, Faulkner would recognize Oxford today; underneath its glossy surface lives the passion and grief of a new generation of writers and artists who have succeeded him.

To those looking at Mississippi's literary landscape from the outside, there exists a belief that Southern literature is all about loss and that Southern writers—particularly Faulkner—believe that what is lost is more valuable than what is gained. In fact, that could not be further from the truth. Faulkner wrote about change more than he wrote about loss, whether it was race and the post–World War II era in *Intruder in the Dust* or the Southern way of death in *As I Lay Dying*. Perhaps Faulkner is misunderstood because of a line from his character Gavin Stevens in *Requiem for a Nun*: "The past is never dead. It's not even past." Many believe this is just Southern shorthand for holding on to an old way of life, when what Faulkner meant was that we should all see the connections between past and present so that their relationship with history can become more clearly visible. Faulkner believed in the power of the past but he did not believe in being imprisoned by it.

Faulkner's relationship to the geography and landscape of his hometown—and the South itself—is complex. "I'm inclined to think that my material, the South, is not very important to me," Faulkner once wrote in a 1944 letter to literary critic Malcolm Cowley. "I just happen to know it, and don't have time in one life to learn another one and write at the same time." While there is much around Oxford that evokes the town of Jefferson and Yoknapatawpha County, the actual places are an amalgam of the North Mississippi Hills and the Delta. You can't just take one of Faulkner's maps of his imagined literary land, impose it on Oxford and Lafayette County, and expect everything to match up. Faulkner effectively moves pieces of the Delta into Yoknapatawpha County, and he does this to a great degree in four novels: *Big Woods*, *Absalom, Absalom!*, *Go Down, Moses*, and *The Wild Palms*. Faulkner's mythic Big Woods is a mixture of places he knew in rural Lafayette County blended with the landscape of the Delta.

Even though the landscape Faulkner wrote about and experienced has changed, there are connections to it that are hiding in plain sight in the shadows of the present. Off a dirt road in rural Lafayette County sits a hunting camp Faulkner once owned, a place where interestingly enough he thought he would raise mules, despite the coming ubiquity of the tractor by local farmers. Off another road you can find the setting for the river crossing in *As I Lay Dying*. As Faulkner scholar Ann Abadie once told me, these things are on the landscape; you just have to know where to look.

Place and nature were important to Faulkner, but so was the built environment. It is in physical spaces from the past, often overshadowed by Oxford's newer, more modern buildings, that visitors to Oxford can get a sense of Faulkner's world. While I was a student at Ole Miss—as the University of Mississippi was nicknamed—in the 1970s, the Meek-Duvall House on University Avenue was known as the "A Rose for Emily" house since it was where Faulkner wrote the classic Southern gothic story. It's still there today, appropriately with a pair of mannequins—they appear

A view of the Yocona River, a site thought to be the inspiration for the river crossing of the Bundren family in William Faulkner's *As I Lay Dying*.

The Meek-Duvall House, or the "A Rose for Emily" house. BELOW The Thompson-Chandler House.

to be stand-ins for the corpse of Miss Emily Grierson—overlooking the street on the balcony in various outfits. Similarly, because of a connection between the real and imagined, the Thompson-Chandler House on South 13th Street is sometimes referred to as the Compson House since Edwin Chandler, who once lived there, so closely resembled Benjy Compson from *The Sound and the Fury*. A small Victorian building just off the Square on Jackson Avenue was the law office of Faulkner's friend, one he placed in the Quentin section of *The Sound and the Fury*: "We went down the street and turned into a bit of lawn, in which, set back from the street, stood a one-storey building of brick trimmed with white. We went up . . . to the door and entered a bare room smelling of stale tobacco."

Yes, Faulkner's world exists throughout Oxford. You just have to know where to look.

✤

ON A SMALL SIDE STREET IN OXFORD stands the regal neoclassical home that once belonged to local physician John Culley and his wife, Nina. It was here that, after a brief correspondence, William Faulkner met Eudora Welty for the first time. The link between the two writers started with a hastily typed letter filled with inaccuracies.

On a piece of unadorned stationery dated April 27, 1943, in an envelope with a Hollywood postmark, William Faulkner wrote a letter to Eudora Welty. "Dear Welty," it began, "You are doing fine. You are doing all right. I read THE GILDED SIX BITS, a friend loaned me THE ROBBER BRIDEGROOM, I just bought the collection named GREEN something, haven't read it yet, expect nothing from it because I expect from you[sic]. You are doing fine. Is there any way that I can help you?"

Oddly enough, William Faulkner confused Eudora Welty with Zora Neale Hurston, which did not upset Welty in the least. But "GREEN something" *was* Welty's story collection *A Curtain of Green*. Welty simply

159

It was here on Sardis Lake that William Faulkner once took Eudora Welty sailing.

described the letter to friends as "strange stuff." In spite of the letter's odd tone, Welty was heartened by the praise from Faulkner, a writer she had long admired. Interestingly enough, Welty never sought Faulkner's help.

They only met on four occasions, and on those few occasions they never discussed literature. "I certainly wasn't going to bring it up," Welty recalled years later. Instead, in the summer of 1949 they sailed together in Faulkner's boat on Sardis Lake, took in the landscape of Mississippi's Hill Country, and gathered at the Culley's house in Oxford for dinner of quail with a group that included Welty's friend Ella Somerville, a grande dame of Oxford society who arranged their meeting. After dinner, the group sang hymns together in an irreverent manner surrounding a Steinway baby grand piano. They didn't need to discuss literature; Faulkner did not want an acolyte and Welty already had a strong sense of the type of writer she wanted to be. Still their work is tied together in the minds of readers as well as literary scholars. Though Welty's fiction rarely has the gothic quality of Faulkner's work, what the two writers had in common is that the lives and actions of their characters remain inexorably linked with the sensory experience of the Mississippi landscape.

Beginning with a 1949 letter to the *New Yorker*, Welty wrote regularly about her fellow Mississippian and his work. When Edmund Wilson said that Faulkner's "weakness has also its origin in the antiquated community he inhabits"—meaning Mississippi—Eudora Welty wrote in defense of Faulkner. "Such critical irrelevance, favorable or unfavorable, the South has long been used to, but now Mr. Wilson fancies it up and it will resound a little louder. Mr. Faulkner all the while continues to be capable of passion, of love, of wisdom, perhaps of prophecy, toward his material. Isn't that enough?"

Faulkner remained remarkably taciturn about Welty's defense and her other writings on his work. Little correspondence turns up until the last time Welty and Faulkner were together on May 24, 1962, when Welty presented Faulkner with the Gold Medal for Fiction from the American Academy of Arts and Letters in New York. It was Faulkner's last trip outside of Mississippi, and in deference to the recipient, Welty gave Faulkner his medal privately before going to the stage and presented only the empty case in the public ceremony.

Although the photograph was probably captured in a tense moment, judging from their facial expressions, once Welty was free of the object that caused her to appear with guarded detachment on camera, she relaxed and gave an elegant tribute to Faulkner. Again, in deference to Faulkner, Welty spoke of him not as a fellow writer in her remarks, but as a reader of his fiction. "The most evident thing in all our minds at this moment," Welty noted to Faulkner and the audience, "must be that your fictional world, with its tragedy, its beauty, its hilarity, its long passion, its generations of feeling and knowing, the whole of your extraordinary world, is alive and in the room here and with us now. We inhabit it; and so will they, each one for himself, the readers in days to come."

The speech Faulkner gave following Welty's introduction was equally memorable. Faulkner said, "This award has, to me, a double value. It is not only a comforting recognition of some considerable years of reasonably hard and arduous, anyway consistently dedicated, work. It also recognizes and affirms, and so preserves, a quantity in our American legend and dream well worth preserving." Faulkner concluded by saying, "Let the past abolish the past when—and if—it can substitute something better; not us to abolish the past simply because it was."

Almost six weeks later Faulkner was dead and Eudora Welty was enlisted to write his obituary for the Associated Press. In that tribute, Welty wrote, "William Faulkner saw all the world in his fictional county where we can see it now—where he made it live. His work is a triumphant vision. This vision, like life itself, has its light and dark, its time and place, and love and battle, its generations of feeling, and its long reaches of what happens to people out there and inside, in heart and mind, which is so much. . . . He went out on every limb, I believe, that he knew was there."

In a letter to Malcolm Cowley, whose publication of *The Portable Faulkner* in 1946 many believe resurrected Faulkner's career, Faulkner had written, "It is my ambition to be, as a private individual, abolished and voided from history, leaving it markless, no refuse save the printed books." If you walk around the Square and read this passage from his novel *Sartoris*, you realize how much of Faulkner's world still exists on this landscape: "The hill flattened away into the plateau on which the town proper had been built these hundred years and more ago, and the street became definitely urban presently with garages and small shops with merchants in shirt sleeves, and customers; the picture show with its lobby plastered with life episodic in colored lithographed mutations. Then the Square, with its unbroken low skyline of old weathered brick and fading dead names stubborn yet beneath scaling paint, and drying Negroes in casual and careless O.D. garments worn by both sexes, and country people in occasional khaki too; and the brisket urbanites weaving among their placid chewing unhaste and among the men in tilted chairs before the stores."

William Faulkner's statue on Oxford's Courthouse Square.

Faulkner has not been voided from history or the place that inspired him. He lives on and when you walk the streets of Oxford, you are walking beside him and walking through the setting of the fictional world he created.

☙

ALTHOUGH OXFORD IS MOST CLOSELY identified with William Faulkner, it is a town that has connections to other parts of Mississippi's literary heritage. Novelist, playwright, scholar, and *New Republic* theater critic Stark Young attended the University of Mississippi and lived part of his early formative years in a Victorian house that still stands today. Young wrote four novels set in Mississippi, his best known being the Civil War saga *So Red the Rose*, published in 1934, which in some ways mirrors his essay "Not in Memoriam, but in Defense," published in the Agrarian manifesto *I'll Take My Stand*. The novel is a romantic view of plantation life before, during, and after the Civil War. "I want it to be a monument in the South of a certain quality of society that was there, in the planting class," which is how Young described his novel in correspondence just one year before its publication. Young, like his fellow agrarians John Crowe Ransom and Allen Tate, believed that the South's past—particularly its antebellum past—was a sacrament and that the region must reject the industrialism of the North. Although Young argued in his essay that the South "can never go back," he also believed that Southern civilization contained many "worthwhile things" that ought to be preserved, particularly a society based on land, family, and tradition.

By the 1960s, both the South's traditions and the very idea of "Southern civilization" were being questioned, particularly the system of Jim Crow segregation that had been baked into the fabric of Southern life for generations. The integration of the University of Mississippi in 1962 by

The Lyceum Building at the University of Mississippi.

James Meredith exposed social and cultural cracks in the South's romanticized idea of itself. Ole Miss has always been a place that took pride in its traditions, and in 1962 the tradition of segregation was shattered by the changes brought about by the civil rights movement. Changing Ole Miss's traditions led to fiery segregationist rhetoric by then-governor Ross Barnett, followed by rioting and violence, two deaths, and federal troops, brought in to keep the peace, driving through Oxford's Square. In their immediate aftermath—and for many years after—the Ole Miss riots were confronted with only silence, and that silence was used as a means of shifting the narrative away from a shameful event rather than confronting it. In the South silence about difficult topics is a preferred method of social control, but that was beginning to change as well.

History professor James W. Silver had observed and analyzed Mississippi's racially repressive culture, including the integration of Ole Miss or what he described as "the great confrontation and its aftermath," since his arrival at the University of Mississippi in 1936. Using his own notes and correspondence and his background as a historian, Silver wrote *Mississippi: The Closed Society* to break the deafening silence that came after the Ole Miss riots. Published during Mississippi's Freedom Summer in 1964, Silver's book provided a much-needed window into the psyche of Southern segregationists and continues, to this day, to be a powerful metaphor for Southern exceptionalism. Silver's idea of Mississippi as a place lacking "the moral resources to reform itself," as well as his speaking out on issues of race, led to harassment, his being ostracized by colleagues, as well as state officials calling for his firing, in spite of his having tenure. Eventually, fearing for the safety of his family, Silver left Oxford and the university. His opponents felt his exile would in time erase his influence, but his words and memory live on. Today there is a pond on campus dedicated to his memory and his personal papers are preserved in the special collections of the university library.

James Silver held an understanding in common with his acquaintance William Faulkner: writers write against orthodoxy. Silver soon learned that pushing against the establishment had a price and was publicly excoriated for speaking his mind. As an insider Faulkner could skewer local culture and tradition, but a perceived outsider like Silver could not. Given Silver's public example of the price of defying orthodoxy—either politically or artistically—it is little wonder that one is hard pressed to think of any other writers who left their mark on Oxford in the decade after Faulkner's death in 1962. But toward the end of the 1970s, a change had begun to take place. There were several forces that created that change, but there are two that are central to Oxford reclaiming the literary legacy William Faulkner left behind: the opening of the independent bookstore Square Books and the creation of the Center for the Study of Southern Culture at the University of Mississippi—the first center devoted to academic study of the region. When both of these establishments opened their doors in 1979, they took risks and began to reclaim and reimagine Oxford and Mississippi's place in the firmament of Southern letters.

By the late 1960s, there was not a single bookstore in the town of Oxford and not a single place in town to purchase a book written by native son William Faulkner. When Richard Howorth returned to his hometown of Oxford in 1979, he decided to change that by opening Square Books in a small storefront owned by a relative right on the town square. "The presence of Rowan Oak and William Faulkner is part of the DNA of this bookstore," Howorth told me one afternoon on the restored balcony of the old Blaylock's Drug Store, which is the store's flagship location. The building is painted a now iconic, attention-getting orange, but the old "Fortune's Famous Ice Cream" sign that would have been familiar to William Faulkner on strolls around the Square is still there. "Faulkner wouldn't recognize the place," Howorth told me, "but he would not be surprised that we are here."

Since its opening in 1979, Square Books has played a significant role in the cultural life of Oxford and the University of Mississippi. "Faulkner wouldn't recognize the place," owner Richard Howorth notes, "but he would not be surprised that we are here."

When Howorth and his wife, Lisa, moved back to Oxford with the idea of opening a bookstore, the Square still had small shops with mom-and-pop merchants in shirtsleeves, much as Faulkner described the merchants of the town of Jefferson in his novels. "There were four drugstores, two hardware stores, two dry cleaners, one grocery store, and two restaurants, one of which served alcohol," Howorth told me. Now all of those businesses are gone and Howorth's bookstore is located in one of those old drugstores. It moved to its current location in 1986 and also has three other locations in Oxford Square, one of which houses rare books and first editions. Although Richard Howorth would never say so, his bookstore has become as much of a tourist attraction as Rowan Oak. And how that happened can be attributed to an assemblage of people who paved the way and were part of Oxford's renaissance. Beginning in the mid-1970s, a special alchemy of people, events, and circumstances helped bring about a cultural shift.

A few years before Square Books opened, Ron Shapiro decided to open his art house theater the Hoka. Back in 1975, Shapiro found an old cotton warehouse just off the Square with no plumbing or wiring as well as a ready band of volunteers and investors. "It was just as community as community can be," Shapiro told me just three months before he died in 2019. "The theater was something people wanted: we got theater seats donated, wood, and investors who just volunteered to put their money into the project." The theater opened the day before Mardi Gras in 1976 with a total investment of eleven thousand dollars and was a mainstay in Oxford for twenty years. As an Ole Miss student it was at the Hoka that I first saw classic films such as *Harold and Maude* and *The Rocky Horror Picture Show*, as well as a few risqué X-rated films shown at midnight that came to be the source of income that kept the Hoka's lights on and allowed them to show art films in limited runs. In the community tradition of the Hoka, Shapiro, known to all in Oxford as Ronzo, even loaned me a print of Ken Russell's *Women in Love* for a private screening for members of the English honor society.

The community engagement and success surrounding the opening of the Hoka was a sign to Richard and Lisa Howorth that Oxford could support a bookstore. To mark the opening of the bookstore they needed an event, but at the time publishers were only sending writers to major media markets. That is why the first event Square Books held was not one that came through the publicity department of a publisher, but from a family connection. In the fall of 1979 Mississippi writer Ellen Douglas had just published her novel *The Rock Cried Out*, and Howorth asked her to conduct the inaugural reading at Square Books since she had been a college classmate and sorority sister of his mother's. It took a few years for publishers to begin to send writers to Square Books. The establishment of the Center for the Study of Southern Culture, its director William Ferris, and a new writer in residence at the University by the name of Willie Morris eventually helped generate events that made Square Books a cultural hub. To help the bookstore, and to add to the cultural life of the university, Ferris, Morris, and Howorth all drew on contacts from beyond the confines of Mississippi.

In 1979, when writer, scholar, and folklorist Bill Ferris became the founding director of the Center for the Study of Southern Culture at the University of Mississippi, a Southerner was in the White House and *Time* magazine, in their September 1976 issue, had deemed the South a region with "implications for the future of America." Given renewed interest in the cultural impact of the American South, the timing was perfect for such a center. And what better place to have it than in a town, state, and university many think of as emblematic of the South.

Ferris arrived in Oxford with an encyclopedic knowledge of Mississippi blues, Southern folk art and culture, and an extensive list of contacts that would rival a Hollywood talent agent. The list included not just fellow Southerners, but anyone interested in the food, life, and culture of the South, with musicians like B. B. King to writers and scholars like Robert Penn Warren, poet Etheridge Knight, and future Pulitzer Prize–winning novelist Alice Walker. Never one to focus exclusively on high culture, Ferris's fundraising for the center included a three-minute film called "Hush, Hoggies, Hush" that features a Mississippi farmer who taught his pigs to pause in prayer before he feeds them. "It turned out to be the most famous thing we ever did because it is something about the farmer reciting and chanting a prayer as these pigs wait, anxious to eat," Ferris told me with a chuckle in his voice. "But they wait and then he says 'Amen' and they eat. It never ceases to bring the house down." It also got people to open their checkbooks, since it was this film that Ferris often used to raise money for the center.

While Ferris's contacts were universal and democratic, former *Harper's* editor Willie Morris brought a Rolodex of boldface literary names from New York when he became writer in residence at the University of Mississippi in January 1980. After years away from Mississippi, Morris was reluctant to return, but was encouraged by friends Larry Wells and Larry's

Willie Morris and his beloved black Lab, Pete, at work.

171

wife, Dean Faulkner Wells, the niece of William Faulkner. By the fall of 1979, Wells said that he and friends had raised the money for Morris's salary and the chancellor of the university had offered him the position. To assuage Morris's reluctance, the Wells invited Morris to a home football game and the camaraderie of game day seemed to quell some of his fears of returning to the South.

Although originally brought to the university by the English department, Morris eventually moved to the department of journalism, a place he felt more fitting for a storyteller and former magazine and newspaper editor. He taught creative writing classes and shared insights with his students on the craft of writing from the perspective of his time as an editor and writer rather than within the confines of literary history. To teach his classes he brought writers such as William Styron, George Plimpton, James Dickey, and Irwin Shaw to meet his students, and many of them also paid a visit to Square Books while they were in town and did a reading.

By the mid-1980s, between book publicity stops made with publishers, events cosponsored by the Center for the Study of Southern Culture, and Willie Morris's friends, Square Books was doing a regular series of readings. Around the same time, a young lawyer from the Memphis suburb of Southaven, Mississippi, became a regular at these readings. John Grisham, a recent graduate of the Ole Miss law school, made a regular eighty-mile trek to Oxford for events. "A lawyer buddy and I would tell our secretaries that we were headed to Oxford to take depositions, or to search land titles, or to pursue some vague activity in federal court, and we'd go to Square Books for coffee and a book signing. We enjoyed meeting the writers on tour." This was about the time Grisham had started writing his first novel, *A Time to Kill*. "I remember daydreaming of my own book signings at some of those readings," Grisham told me. When *A Time to Kill* was published in 1989, Grisham called Richard Howorth about doing a book event and he said yes. A lot of bookstores had turned him down, which is why Square Books is one of the few bookstores that does a book signing tied to the release of each new thriller by John Grisham. Grisham still remembers that he sold fifty books at his first signing, which he says was "a respectable number."

As an observer of Oxford's growth as a literary town, he says, "There were several important events that prompted the literary renaissance in Oxford. First, and by far the most important, was the opening of Square Books in 1979. Next was the return to Mississippi of Willie Morris in 1980 and his decision to live, teach, and write in Oxford. Next into the cultural mix was Barry Hannah."

If Willie Morris focused on the beauty, manners, and sensibilities of the South in his writing, as well as a straightforwardness in his prose, novelist and short story writer Barry Hannah was known for his raucous characters, furious energy, and postmodern Faulknerian complexities. "The Deep South might be wretched, but it can howl," Hannah wrote in his story "Ride, Fly, Penetrate, Loiter." As a hard-drinking, gun-toting man from Clinton, Mississippi, Barry Hannah was known in the literary world for howling louder than a southbound freight train. When Hannah arrived in 1982, his editor, Seymour Lawrence, had already taken up part-time residence in Oxford and lived in a house across from Rowan Oak with his partner, the novelist Joan Williams, who once had a relationship with William Faulkner as a young woman.

With the specter of Mississippi's closed society being a thing of the past, by the late 1980s the literary and artistic community of Oxford had grown into a small, tightly knit group, much like in the days of William Faulkner. It would seem as if this small spot in the South had reached a critical mass of literary talent. But the reason for placing writers in residence at universities and university towns is to help build the next generation of practitioners of the craft. "The attraction to being a writer can only strengthen if you are in contact with writers while you are coming of

173

NOT EVEN PAST

age, which lets you know that being a writer is something you can aspire to become," JoAnne Prichard Morris, a former university press editor and the widow of Willie Morris, told me when asked about what she felt was Willie's legacy at Ole Miss. As Morris and Hannah began to teach writing, they also began to encourage the most talented of their students. One day Morris went to Hannah and said, "Hannah, I got a little genius for you." Future Pulitzer Prize winner for fiction Donna Tartt was then a freshman from the Delta town of Greenville but was soon admitted to Hannah's graduate workshop. "She was well-read; all she needed was life and a story," Hannah told the *Paris Review* in 2004. "Just a rare genius, really. A literary star."

Like Donna Tartt, Oxford fireman Larry Brown was well-read, but began by devouring all the works of western writer Louis L'Amour and page-turners by Harold Robbins rather than the classics Donna Tartt had read. Through his visits to Square Books, Brown soon turned his attention to the stories of Raymond Carver and Flannery O'Connor, as well as essays on the craft of writing, most notably O'Connor's *Mystery and Manners*. Eventually he took a class in fiction writing from Barry Hannah. Initially Hannah was not impressed. "When I first met him, I was struck by his personal commitment," Hannah told the *New York Times* in 1990, "but at the time I didn't give him a prayer, I really didn't think he had it." In just four years after studying with Hannah, Brown published a collection of stories called *Facing the Music* and the novel *Dirty Work*. Hannah said that Brown had "become one of America's great stories—how his diligence and his big backbone won out. Something happened in about five years that's quite a miracle. He's become his own genius."

Larry Brown brought into focus the rough and gritty South that lived outside the confines of genteel Oxford and the Greek columns that dominate the campus of the University of Mississippi. Brown may have refined his craft in the classroom and by reading the work of great Southern writers, but his work remains true to the part of rural Mississippi that shaped

Novelist Larry Brown brought into focus the working-class South
that existed outside the confines of genteel Oxford.

him. It's something that shines through in his memoir *On Fire*, which has
a subtitle that describes exactly what the book is about: *A Personal Account
of Life and Death and Choices*. *On Fire* is an unromantic view of what life is
like as a firefighter in a small Southern town, and the trauma he and his
fellow firefighters face is not sugarcoated. After reading *On Fire*, you realize that the people he writes about in his fiction are people he knows. His
novel *Fay*, the story of a woman moving from the Mississippi Hill Country
with two dollars to her name, even seems to be in conversation with the
characters from Jesmyn Ward's *Sing, Unburied, Sing*, who travel the same
highways and landscape, but from south to north Mississippi. Reading
the two books together it's clear that both writers have a gift for dialogue
and place, and it seems as if the two are making a pilgrimage up and down
the state.

A winter landscape in Mississippi Hill Country, outside of Oxford.

The nine stories that make up Brown's collection *Big Bad Love* are all told from a first-person point of view, and the writing is raw and honest, a reflection of Brown's ear for dialogue. "Love was a big word and it covered a lot of territory," one of Brown's characters opines during a moment of reflection in the title story. "You could spend your whole life chasing after it and wind up with nothing, be an old bitter guy with long nose hair and ear hair and no teeth, hanging out in bars, looking for somebody your age, but the chances of success went down then. After a while you got too many strikes against you."

If the 1980s marked the blossoming of Oxford's literary renaissance, the 1990s brought it into full flower. John Grisham witnessed both decades first as an observer and later as a participant. Although he sold a healthy fifty copies of *A Time to Kill* at his first event at Square Books in 1989, he sold a thousand copies when his blockbuster *The Firm* was released in 1991. By 1993 Grisham endowed a writer-in-residence program for emerging writers and several years later purchased the home of the late editor Seymour Lawrence as a place to house the writers. The writer-in-residence program has helped build the faculty of the Masters of Fine Arts in Creative Writing program at the university, which now includes former writers in residence Tom Franklin; his wife and Mississippi poet laureate, Beth Ann Fennelly; Kiese Laymon; and Aimee Nezhukumatathil; as well as novelists Chris Offutt, Matt Bondurant, and Melissa Ginsburg; and poets Ann Fisher Wirth and Derrick Harriell. Other Mississippi writers who have been Grisham Writers in Residence include Steve Yarbrough, Mary Miller, Brad Watson, and Jesmyn Ward.

Grisham shies away from the label "literary philanthropist" that some have foisted on him. "I'm not sure I know what a literary philanthropist really is," he told me. "Sure, the royalties allow me to be generous to the MFA program. But the freedom allows me to be generous with time."

Grisham's freedom also inspired him to help bail out the fledgling *Oxford American*, a literary magazine that published its first issue in Oxford, Mississippi, in 1992. The first issue of the *Oxford American* was eclectic and quirky, with a story by Richard Ford, a poem by John Updike about a bowel movement, and an interview with film critic Pauline Kael, and every writer for the first issue received no payment for the publication of their work. "People here are bored and disgusted," founding editor Marc Smirnoff wrote in his declaration of intent for the first issue of the magazine, "with the sentimental and clichéd depictions of the South that are rerun in the so-called Southern magazines of record." He went further to note that the *Oxford American* "will not publish pieces about family reunions, or recipes, or beauty contests, or picturesque porches, or local anchormen, or picnicking, or interior decorating, or lovely gardens, or Southern soap opera stars."

Financed largely by founding editor Smirnoff's credit cards and loans from family and friends, the magazine billed as "the Southern magazine of good writing" ceased publication in 1994 but was resuscitated by an infusion of cash by Grisham. "It was as simple as helping a friend in need," Grisham remarked about his support of the *Oxford American*. "I'd met Marc Smirnoff at Square Books and was happy to contribute to his early editions of the *Oxford American*. Then one day the *OA* was in a real bind, so I wrote a check. Then another. Over the next ten years I wrote a lot of checks and burned some cash, but I have no regrets." Although it is no longer published in Mississippi, Grisham says, "It is still a great magazine."

TODAY IT IS HARD to walk the streets of Oxford without running into a writer or a student who aspires to be a writer. If it is true that in order for someone to become a writer it helps to encounter writers in one's day-to-day life, Oxford is the place to be. The creative writing program at the

A gathering of members of Oxford's writing community on the steps of Rowan Oak. From left to right, front: Dustin Parsons, Lisa Howorth, Melissa Ginsburg, Ann Fisher-Wirth, Alysia Burton Steele, Beth Ann Fennelly, Jaime Harker, Sarah Frances Hardy, Aimee Nezhukumatathil; middle: Mary Miller, Derrick Harriell, Tucker Carrington, Tom Franklin, Jemar Tisby; back: Chris Offutt, William Boyle, Ace Atkins, Curtis Wilkie, Adam Gussow, Ted Ownby, Charles Reagan Wilson, Jim Dees, Kiese Laymon, R. J. Lee, Matt Bondurant, David Crews, W. Ralph Eubanks, Julian Randall, Michael Farris Smith, Charlie Spillers.

University of Mississippi has grown and is thriving; regular literary events at Square Books and on the university campus attract students, members of the Oxford community, and its community of writers. That community of writers has grown from William Faulkner in the first half of the twenti-eth century to a small handful of talent in the 1980s to nearly forty work-ing writers today, including journalists and creative nonfiction humorists, poets, and novelists of every stripe. The bar at City Grocery is a gathering

179

NOT EVEN PAST

spot for local writers, several of whom have a brass plate at the bar with their name and drink of choice engraved on it. A signed portrait of writer Larry Brown sits in a place of honor behind the bar.

Ronzo Shapiro will more than likely gain a shrine behind the bar, more for his love and support of literature in Oxford than for being a writer. Up until his death in August 2019, Ronzo attended almost every reading at Square Books, which may be why on the night he died every writer in Oxford who could make it gathered at the City Grocery bar to reflect on his life and how he supported writing and promoted reading. Everyone remembered that when a writer ascended the stairs to City Grocery after a reading, they were greeted by the whirr of his whistle, which gave off a sound associated more with the circus than a literary event. The whistle seemed like a random gimmick, but what I believe Ron Shapiro understood by that action was that literature is performance. City Grocery is where one loses ones artistic persona and becomes just another human being at the public bar foot rail. As Ronzo was quick to remind everyone,

This dogtrot house outside of Oxford would have been a typical sight in William Faulkner's rural Mississippi hill country.

The cedar-lined path leading to Rowan Oak.

even the author of the grimmest memoirs, "It's never too late to have a happy childhood."

The shadows of past writers who have lived in Oxford—Willie Morris, Barry Hannah, Larry Brown, William Faulkner—loom large but the current group of writers who make Oxford home is eclectic and varied, and not all of them were born in Mississippi or even in the South. But these are people who have chosen to make Mississippi their home and they embrace it as strongly and passionately as any native. Poet Aimee Nezhukumatathil, who came to Mississippi from New York as a Grisham Writer in Residence, begins her poem "My South" by noting, "My south started with sugar / boiled and spilled for birds / green as my mom's signature ring," revealing her growing connection to Mississippi as a place. By the time the poem concludes, she notes the comfort and relief of a sense of belonging, one so strong that "even on my first day, never asked / if I'm from around here or just visiting."

The Hill Country symbolizes the reality of the Magnolia State, with a variety of terrains that roll up and down, with vast gullies sometimes filled with untamed kudzu vines. Once you leave the hills surrounding Oxford and head west toward the Mississippi River, the terrain begins to flatten. The hills in this part of Hill Country are not dramatic in appearance, just bumpy spots that look like a blanket thrown over an unmade bed. But once those bumps begin to spread out across the horizon the land signals that you have arrived in the Delta, a place that represents Mississippi in the popular imagination, with its romanticized hardscrabble life and seemingly endless fields of cotton. But the Delta is also a place where the romance and reality of Mississippi begin to collide, and that conflict plays out in the literature that has its origins in the region or is inspired by it.

CHAPTER SIX

The hills of Mississippi Hill Country tend to roll and gently flatten.

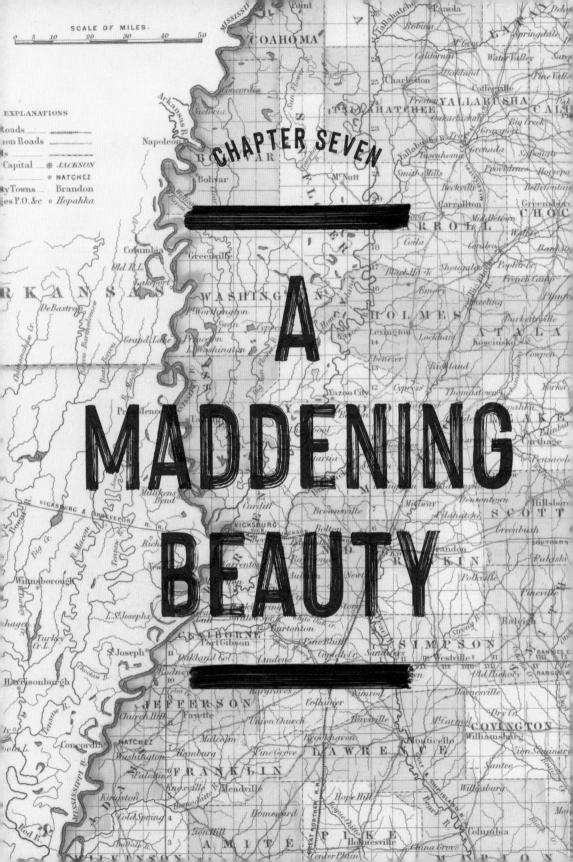

CHAPTER SEVEN

A MADDENING BEAUTY

The Delta is very rich and visually striking, but completely flat. I would find it maddening after days with nothing but the horizon. Just before you reach it, there are high bluffs, and to get in you plunge down a deep hill, and from then on there's nothing but flatness.

—Eudora Welty, in a 1972 interview
with *The Paris Review*

Sunrise over a field in the Mississippi Delta.

WITHIN THE BOUNDARIES of the fictional Yoknapatawpha County is a piece of land called the Big Woods. While this spot on Faulkner's map of his fictional universe lies in Mississippi's Hill Country, the Big Woods was actually inspired by the landscape of the Mississippi Delta. The description of the Big Woods in "The Bear" as a "doomed wilderness whose edges were being constantly and punily gnawed at by men with plows and axes" mirrors the clearing of the Delta by lumbermen in the late nineteenth and early twentieth centuries. In that same story, Ike McCaslin—a significant figure in several Faulkner stories—discovers that in the Big Woods a man has to get lost to find himself, much like early settlers of the Delta. McCaslin finds himself in this setting again on his last hunt in "Delta Autumn," a story in which Faulkner describes the Big Woods as "bigger and older than any recorded document." That is the way Mississippians view the Delta: bigger and older than time itself. If the Gulf Coast and the Piney Woods are places in Mississippi that exist outside the Southern myth, the Delta is the living embodiment of that mythology.

Faulkner, like most Hill Country people, was obsessed with the Delta. Delta native Willie Morris believed Faulkner needed the "exotic, unregenerate, profligate, hedonistic, tormented Delta" as a counterbalance to his unextravagant hills. That makes sense because there is a severity to the landscape of the Delta that cannot be found anywhere in Hill Country.

The teardrop-shaped expanse of land known as the Mississippi Delta is two hundred miles long and flat as far as the eye can see. At sunset it seems as if the sky consumes the ground that lies beneath it and gives a glowing texture to the wide expanse of fields. The landscape is lush and pastoral, much like the dreamy setting described by Eudora Welty in her novel *Delta Wedding*. Her character Laura McRaven describes the Delta as a place with a "quieting and vanishing of sound" and a sky "the color of violets." The Delta hypnotizes Laura as she takes the train there from Jackson and arrives in this seemingly remote world just before dark. Upon her arrival, the place pierces Laura's consciousness and overtakes her, just as it does for any first-time visitor. Whatever it is, the glow of the Delta at dusk holds the ability to cast a spell, something it has done over quite a few Mississippi writers.

The Delta is one of those rare places that is possible to find both maddening and beautiful. Through my years of traveling this part of the state, I have come to realize that if a place as rich and tortured as the Mississippi Delta did not exist, some raconteur south of the Mason-Dixon Line would have had to make it up. In a world of Southern storytellers, someone would have surely invented a tale of a swampy, seemingly untameable wilderness with dark,

A sky "the color of violets," much like one described by Laura McRaven in Eudora Welty's *Delta Wedding*.

These day laborers, captured by Farm Security Administration photographer Marion Post Wolcott, are beginning a day when they will work "from can to can't," meaning from dawn—when you can see—until darkness, when you cannot.

rich soil that men and women conquered at great cost in order to make the place their own.

And without a doubt storytellers have left their mark on this landscape. You find it in the names of some towns and hamlets that create a patchwork quilt of nomenclature and meaning, in places like Midnight, Alligator, or Panther Burn. Some locales even have their own unique shorthand, like in the town of Moorhead where two railroad lines intersect at a perfect perpendicular angle, which is locally known as where "the Southern crosses the Dog." Almost every town has its own origin story, one that becomes richer and fuller with time. Imagination is stamped into the cultural fabric of the Delta, making it central to Mississippi's literary landscape.

Yet it is difficult to look at the Delta landscape without seeing pain, both past and present. The Delta's story is not just about the sins of the South; it is also a story of America and this country's thirst and ambition for transformation and reinvention. The Delta's story is like the Magnolia State's own version of manifest destiny, one that allowed the state to expand north and west into the richest farmland in North America. It was first settled by planters who—after taming the land—remade the Delta in their own vision and image. And it is the result of that vision that travelers to Mississippi see on the land today, a legacy of the severe and austere economics of sharecropping and a consistently high rate of poverty that remain startlingly visible and cannot be ignored.

Ironically, this is a land of rich soil and poor people, a place where the fields were worked in a period they called "from can to can't," meaning from dawn—when you can see—until darkness, when you can't. Suffering and injustice permeate visions of the Delta landscape as much as the wail of the blues, the musical form inspired by the inequities this rich land inflicted on the black people who labored it. If you asked me to describe the blues, I would say it is sorrow and beauty wrapped together. The blues exists as an art form with an aesthetic sense that finds its center in the loss, longing, joy, and pain of the very landscape that created it.

In spite of the blues, near the dimming of the day a warm light envelops this southern plain. At dusk, the sky above the fields of the Mississippi Delta glow with red and orange as if it were a fireplace. Maybe it is the expansiveness of the land that creates this light, but whatever it is, for a brief part of the day beauty soothes the echo of the ghostlike weary blues that seem to howl and scream across this wide and often empty berth of land.

When Mississippi became a state in 1817, the Delta was firmly in the hands of the Choctaw Indians. Of course, the Indians were removed from the land and subsequently white settlers arrived between 1825 and 1827. For settlers, a move into what was once called the Yazoo Bottoms to farm its rich soil presented the chance to make a fortune, but given the labor required to clear the land, it required a lot of money and a lot of slaves before that fortune could be made. This was not a place for a thrifty farmer with a strong work ethic and a dream. Writer and Mississippian David Cohn once commented that the Delta was settled by "pioneers with means," people of sizeable wealth who had the means to shoulder a great deal of risk. In some parts of the Delta, the average white family owned more than eighty slaves. By 1860 the slave population was nearly five times the size of its white population, an imbalance that in time bred racial distrust and discomfort. After emancipation that black population became sharecroppers.

Nostalgia abounds in stories of the antebellum South—even in the poorest regions—with tales of great wealth in those years. In the case of the Mississippi Delta, its residents did improve their fortunes within a short period of time and were affluent enough to live what many would call "the good life." Greenwood LeFlore—Choctaw chieftain and owner of approximately four hundred slaves—in 1855 ordered ten thousand dollars' worth of furnishings from France for a single room in his house. Similar tales of opulence and excess are part of the story, in spite of few signs of affluence today.

The way most people think of the Mississippi Delta is the romantic version, a world described by Ellen Gilchrist's stories of the dying Delta aristocracy in *In the Land of Dreamy Dreams* and by writers like Tennessee Williams, William Alexander Percy, and Shelby Foote of privileged families and a world of noblesse oblige. The Cutrer Mansion in Clarksdale is a living monument to this world, with its grand ballroom and vast yard where attorney J. W. Cutrer and his wife, Blanche, daughter of Clarksdale founder John Clark, hosted opulent parties attended by a young Tennessee Williams. The mansion and those parties subsequently inspired characters and settings of *A Streetcar Named Desire*, *The Glass Menagerie*, *Orpheus Descending*, and *Cat on a Hot Tin Roof*. But there is a harsh and hardened version of the Delta, a place often visited by tragedy wrought by the elements, something Eudora Welty realized when she created the sheltered pastoral setting of Shellmound Plantation. Welty said she "made a careful investigation to find the year in which nothing very terrible had happened in the Delta by way of floods or fires or wars that would have taken the men away. I settled it by the almanac." The book is set in 1923, when Welty would have been a little girl, which is why she allows the character of Laura at nine years old to be an observer of part of the narrative.

In many ways, the Delta represents the way Mississippi likes to think of itself in spite of evidence to the contrary: rich and with limitless resources. In a land that poet and planter William Alexander Percy described as one that "lies flat, like a badly drawn half oval," the topsoil rests up to thirty-five feet into the earth in some parts. The plantation economy boomed in the 1850s, leading the state geologist of Mississippi to predict that within a century "whatever the Delta of the Nile once may have been, will only be a shadow of what the alluvial plain of the Mississippi River will then be. It will be the centre-point—the garden spot of the North

The Cutrer Mansion once hosted opulent parties attended by a young Tennessee Williams. Those parties and the setting inspired memorable characters and settings of Williams's plays.

American continent—where wealth and prosperity culminate." That is why Tennessee Williams has his character Big Daddy make a similar proclamation to his son Brick in *Cat on a Hot Tin Roof*. When Big Daddy remarks that he owns "twenty-eight thousand acres of the richest land this side of the valley Nile," he forgets that before his land was cleared and settled it was nothing but a fever-infested wilderness. And clearing the land was an overwhelming task, one that seemed unconquerable until the railroads provided the means to transform the place into a cotton kingdom.

Mary Hamilton's autobiography *Trials of the Earth* tells the story of a rougher version of the Delta than often turns up in much of the literature of the region, outside of the blues. Hamilton came to the Delta in 1896 when it was largely a wilderness of virgin timber and canebrakes and captures the making of the modern-day Delta, which was made possible by logging and the railroads. Her description of the Delta when she arrives leaves as strong an impression as an oversized photograph:

> Oak, gum, ash, hackberry, and poplar stood so thick, with no underbrush, only big blue cane growing rank and tall, almost to the limbs of the trees. It looked so odd, but what looked odder still to me was the black mud, "gumbo," Frank said it was. When we came out on the Mississippi River, the ground was sandy, but it was black sand, and the woods were thinner; there were fewer trees but larger—big old cottonwoods and sycamores that seemed to me when I looked up like their tops were lost in the sky.

It was the clearing of the thick forest of trees that Hamilton describes as "lost in the sky" that made way for the long flat vistas of today's landscape. Born just after the Civil War in 1866, Hamilton marries mysterious hard-drinking Englishman Frank Hamilton, who runs a logging camp for men clearing the Delta's primeval forest. Mary Hamilton becomes the chief cook for her husband's logging camp and runs a boarding house in order for the family to survive financially. Her story is one of the few

The flat open vista of this Delta farm was created by the clearing of a thick forest at the end of the nineteenth century.

A MADDENING BEAUTY

first-person accounts by a woman detailing what it took to settle and clear the Delta. Her description of the trials of her life can be both mundane and funny, such as how she describes coping with a flood in 1897 when she is standing in waist-high water in her living room: "There are times in every woman's life when it is a greater relief to swear than to pray. Well, I did both then."

If Hamilton's story of life in the Delta in the early twentieth century is one of hard work, isolation, and sadness, William Alexander Percy and David Cohn examine the Delta from a more patrician perspective. Percy, the son and grandson of Delta planters—his father was a U.S. senator and his grandfather served as a colonel in the Civil War—inherited the mantle left to him but saw himself more as a writer, poet, and patron of the arts in his native Greenville. David Cohn, unlike Percy, was not a member of the landed planter class. Instead, he was the son of Jewish immigrants who moved to Greenville in the 1880s to become dry goods merchants. Yet both men wrote about their native Delta landscape and its people in an attempt to make sense of the place that shaped them, Percy as a member of the landowning elite and Cohn as an expatriate who no longer lived in the Delta. What their writing reveals are the myths and realities of the ways the Delta is perceived, both inside the state and outside of it.

It was David Cohn who famously proclaimed that the "Mississippi Delta begins in the lobby of the Peabody Hotel in Memphis and ends on Catfish Row in Vicksburg." For citizens of the Delta, Cohn believed Memphis glowed "with the beauty of the honey-colored pile" of a Greek temple "seen at sunrise from a high Athenian hill." If the Delta had a capital city, it would be Memphis, a place that served as both a crossroads for the cotton trade and a transitional place for African Americans on their way north during the Great Migration. Richard Wright, in *Black Boy*, described Memphis as "the first lap of my journey to a land where I could live with a little less fear." It was a liminal space, still Southern but just a river crossing of the Mississippi where the idea of the American west began, at least figuratively. For most Delta residents, Memphis was the only city in the region and a place to escape, much like New Orleans for the southern part of the state. But it is a town that is as much a part of Mississippi as it is of Tennessee, which is the point Cohn makes. Once you leave the bright lights of Memphis, the Deep South and the deep down Delta begins. As Greenville-born poet Charles G. Bell writes about Memphis in "The Hills":

> A night in Memphis, then the last stand of the hills
> They veer off east and south with the curved Yazoo,
>
> Return at Vicksburg, closing the Delta bowl—
> Red bluffs and gullied slopes, a leached-out soil
> Of meager farms and men, Hill-billy towns.

If Memphis is the capital of the Delta, the town of Greenville served as the region's literary and cultural center. In addition to poets William Alexander Percy and Charles G. Bell and writer David Cohn, Greenville was the home of Civil War writer Shelby Foote; novelists Walker Percy, Ellen Douglas, and William Attaway; and Pulitzer Prize–winning newspaper editor Hodding Carter II. It is also the hometown of contemporary writers like humorist Julia Reed, novelist and memoirist Beverly Lowry, poet Brooks Haxton, and journalist and commentator Hodding Carter III. Greenville is not a place short on literary talent, yet it is in the life and writing of William Alexander Percy that one can see most clearly how the complexities of place in the Delta inspired him and other Greenville writers to become writers.

The town of Greenville is perched right at a bend of the Mississippi River, a position that connects its residents to that mighty river and also places them at its mercy when its banks overflow. The poetry of William

Alexander Percy often evokes the character and mood of his hometown, with poems such as "In the Delta," "Greenville Trees," and "Levee Nocturne." But it is his memoir, *Lanterns on the Levee: Recollections from a Planter's Son*, on which Percy's literary reputation rests. Published in 1941, just a year before his death, it is a memoir of manners, morals, and aristocratic responsibility, more of an apologia for his life of privilege than a thoughtful examination of it. At the core of the narrative are Percy's memories of the fortunes and misfortunes of life as a Delta planter's son, noting that people of his class have been "fortunate in their misfortunes." While the prose is beautiful in its Victorian evocation of the culture of the white Delta elite, it is Percy's lack of introspection about the aftermath of the Great Flood of 1927 and his defense of white Southern paternalism—which his cousin, novelist Walker Percy, describes as "strong feelings about the shift of power from the virtuous few"—that makes his memoir a period piece rather than a timeless classic of Southern literature.

The Mississippi River near the Delta town of Greenville.

In *Lanterns on the Levee*, Percy describes sharecropping as the best system for giving profits to "the simple and unskilled." Yet he admits that the system left room for dishonesty: "The Negro is no more on an equality with the white man in plantation matters than in any other dealings between the two. The white planter may charge an exorbitant rate of interest, he may allow the share-cropper less than the market price received for his cotton, he may cheat him in a thousand different ways, and the Negro's redress is merely theoretical." Given that this system depended on black labor, it is little wonder that when the Great Flood of 1927 came, Percy's concern was more with maintaining the Delta's pool of black farm labor than with treating the thousands of people, black and white, equally when they were housed in refugee camps after the flood.

Blues singer Bessie Smith provides the best and simplest description of what happened during the 1927 flood in "Back Water Blues": "when it thunders and lightnin' and the wind begins to blow, there's thousands of people ain't got no place to go." The great flood displaced thousands of Delta residents, the majority of them black. During the flood, Percy was in charge of Red Cross relief efforts in Greenville and admitted that he "became a dictator" because of his access to food supplies and transportation. "If I had to be a despot I was very anxious to be a beneficent one," Percy wrote. In Greenville, black residents of the refugee camp complained of rough treatment and discrimination in regard to labor conditions and distribution of food. There were also complaints that whites came and went as they pleased, while blacks were not given similar privileges. Since black refugees were seen as part of the labor pool, Delta planters did not want to allow them to leave.

In spite of Percy's efforts to control the black labor pool, thousands of black Delta residents moved north as part of the Great Migration after the flood. And while from a contemporary perspective Percy's aristocratic attitudes may elicit disdain, it is important to remember that he was a man

A MADDENING BEAUTY

Yazoo City 5-13-27

Refugees of the Great Mississippi River Flood in Yazoo City, May 13, 1927.

who loved the place he was from but felt he was also "the right man in the wrong place." "Poets are always needed but it takes an effort to realize it," he wrote in 1910, "while it takes no effort to see the good a practical man with a passion for righteousness could do here [in the Delta]." Percy was a gay man in the Mississippi Delta, making him a window into two cultural identities: Southern and queer. As a man who felt as if he were in the wrong place and had to repress one of his identities, he may have asserted his patrician white male Southern identity as a way of masking his queerness. In the early twentieth-century culture of the Mississippi Delta, it also would have been impossible for Percy to see a connection between his own struggles to fit into the existing social system with the plight of black Delta residents. Being a planter provided Percy with the means to escape the repressive culture he found himself tied to, which he did frequently, such as "sailing to Japan" after turning over the flood relief efforts to his friend Hazelwood Farish in the summer of 1927.

What is significant about *Lanterns on the Levee* is that it reveals how in the American South writers place parts of their narratives in separate spheres. Percy separates his narrative of the land from the people who work the land, leading the actual story and the discourse around it to become disconnected and dislodged from one another. It is something William Alexander Percy's cousin Walker Percy came to realize when he became a writer. Walker Percy believed that his cousin—the man who adopted him and his brothers after the untimely death of their parents and who he called Uncle Will—would be astonished with the change of the South as it emerged from "its traditional role as loser and scapegoat" and became the setting of the struggle toward black equality. Perhaps Walker Percy could see the way these two narratives connected since the Delta planter tradition was one he observed only after arriving in Greenville as a teenager rather than being born into it. Walker Percy's examination of the

A MADDENING BEAUTY

South existed more in a philosophical realm, one that is apparent in his novels, including *The Moviegoer* and *The Last Gentleman*.

Walker Percy's character Binx Bolling in *The Moviegoer* is restless and uneasy, a man who sees everydayness as the enemy of living a spiritually fulfilled life. Binx, like Percy, is searching for the truth outside himself, with the South as a backdrop to that search. Percy's character Will Barrett in *The Last Gentleman* returns to the South to reckon with the memory of his father's suicide—much like the author himself had to do—and comically fails to adhere to his father's aristocratic mold. It is when Barrett finds himself outside the South and in the more barren setting of the American West that he has a revelation: "Here it was three o'clock but it was not like three o'clock in Mississippi. In Mississippi it is always Wednesday afternoon, or perhaps Thursday." In just two sentences Percy captures the way the Delta landscape has of seducing its people into believing that life flows with an exclusive rhythm, one that exists only in that place and nowhere else.

If the feeling that it is always Wednesday afternoon in the Mississippi Delta is an idiosyncratic perspective on the South, it is this unique way of experiencing life that fuels the creativity of the Delta's writers. Part of the creative fuel for the writer Ellen Douglas were the dueling topics of race and Southern culture and how they functioned in a cultural space like the Delta. When she was awarded a Houghton Mifflin Literary Fellowship for her first novel, *A Family's Affairs*, Josephine Haxton assumed the pseudonym of Ellen Douglas to protect her maternal aunts in the river town of Natchez. A native of Natchez, Douglas's aunts had inspired the story and they consented for Douglas to use the events of their lives as long as they did not have to read about it.

The town of Homochitto stands in for Natchez in *A Family's Affairs* and, similarly, when writing about the Delta, Philippi takes the place of Greenville. When Douglas published "On the Lake," her penetrating story about race that is set in Philippi, in the *New Yorker* in 1961, her pseudonym was blown, at least in literary circles in Greenville. Her friends Betty and Hodding Carter II quickly recognized the boating accident that the story fictionalizes as one that occurred when the author was fishing with her sons.

The story opens with the line "Late summer in Philippi is a deadly time of year" and continues by describing the heat that grips the Delta in the summer. The lake in the story is a perfect description of Greenville's Lake Ferguson, which was formed in a horseshoe-shaped bend of the Mississippi, built to straighten the river's course. The story revolves around a white woman, Anna, who invites a black woman, Estella, to go fishing in a small boat with her sons. Estella was once employed by Anna, and in the course of the story the two women, particularly Anna, seem to be struggling to shift the power dynamic in their relationship. In spite of not having enough life preservers, Anna asks Estella to join them in their boat for a fishing expedition. When the boat capsizes and Estella begins to drown, Anna must confront their relationship. Did she invite Estella to fish just to demonstrate how broad-minded she was? Was Anna's invitation an effort to buy Estella's friendship? Anna kicks Estella away as she tries to save her, and through the physical action Douglas demonstrates the difficulty of white and black relationships at the time, particularly those relationships that were with black domestic help. "On the Lake" put a spotlight on the Southern version of white liberal guilt as it never had been before.

Douglas's son, poet Brooks Haxton, says his memories of the incident that inspired "On the Lake" over the years have been blended somewhat with the written story. Estella was based on the family's former housekeeper, Rosetta, and Brooks Haxton vividly remembers seeing Rosetta having spasms, expelling water from her lungs and gut. What Douglas did with many of the details and facts of an incident from her life was to expand them to create a backstory and dramatic tension. "One deviation from fact is that we got swamped on our way out, when we were about

Greenville's Lake Ferguson, the setting of Ellen Douglas's "On the Lake."

halfway across the lake," Haxton remembers. "So the whole episode of what we did on the sandbar is taken from a general sense of how such outings went rather than the details of that day. When the boat went under, I remember swimming over toward Mama and she raised her voice to shoo me away. I didn't understand that she was holding on to Rosetta underwater." From what Douglas told her son, the details of the boat sinking and her struggle to hold on to Rosetta were very near the actual facts.

In "On the Lake" and in her other stories and novels Ellen Douglas reveals an understanding of how fiction holds the power to shape one's perception of a place and region. She also used people and place to explore hard truths, particularly about race. Douglas once said that over the years she became "more and more interested in what's true and what isn't true and how impossible it is to recognize the truth or to tell the truth or to read a book and know it's true." Perhaps that is why her last book, a memoir, was called *Truth: Four Stories I Am Finally Old Enough to Tell*. For a writer shaped by a land drenched in mythology, Ellen Douglas never stopped seeking out the truth.

THESE IDEAS OF TRUTH, memory, and race came forth from the Delta not just in the written word, but in the blues. There is an old saying, "your blues ain't like mine," meaning the music and lyrics of a blues song are an intensely personal way of expressing pain. For black Delta residents, the blues became a form of self-expression that was simply a part of the emotional equipment of life. The blues is simply poetry wrapped in a struggle for survival. When you place the Delta blues together thematically, the expressions of personal trials and pain form a Homeric, rhythmic epic poem that tell all of the stories this flat expanse of land holds, including a few that have been hidden or masked.

And there were plenty of personal trials and pain in the Delta and in Mississippi. One being a lack of education. Mississippi senator and governor James K. Vardaman denounced the education of an African American as "a positive unkindness that renders him unfit for the work which the white man has prescribed him and which he will be forced to perform." Vardaman's demands as well as the constraints of the Jim Crow system had an unlikely impact: they sparked the artistic creativity of the black people of the Delta. And given that the black residents in the cotton kingdom of the Delta—and those across Mississippi—were deemed unworthy of receiving education and literacy, African American literary writers who emerged out of the Delta did so against great odds. Rather than seeing the Delta land as a thing of beauty, black writers focused on the pain the land inflicted upon them and how they sought to confront and overcome that pain. For these writers the Delta is connected to a consciousness ruptured by memories of pain, theft, and poverty, the same themes that dominate the region's singularly most important art form, the blues.

My introduction to the blues and the struggles of black people in the Delta began on trips I made regularly to the Delta with my father, who came to work in the Delta in 1949 right after graduating with a degree in agronomy from Tuskegee Institute. Once he pointed out an old juke joint he and his friends used to visit; I remember him telling me that the story of Stackalee and Billy seemed to "play out there every Saturday night" with someone getting shot. Then he sang:

> Stackalee went home, got his forty four
> He said "I'm going to the barroom to pay that debt I owe"
>
> Stakalee went to the barroom, stood across the barroom door
> He said, "Don't nobody move." And he pulled his forty-four.

ABOVE Po' Monkey's Lounge was one of the last rural juke joints in Mississippi.
BELOW A sharecropper's home on Marcella Plantation, Mileston.

It was during those visits that my young mind connected the two, the stark landscape and the music of the blues. The Delta to me was another world, one separate and distinct from the one I lived in a mere hundred miles away. My mother also had visions of otherworldliness when she arrived in the Delta in 1952, but for different reasons. Whereas youthful optimism turned my focus toward the landscape and the music that sprang from it, it was the way black people in the Delta lived that caught my mother's attention. The lives she encountered seemed as stark and bereft as the land itself. "I'd never seen poverty like that. People lived in shacks insulated with newspaper and cardboard," she recalled to me once. Hired as a teacher, some of her students lived in those shacks. She arrived at what she thought was the start of the school year, only to learn that school could not begin until the surrounding fields were picked clean of that white gold called cotton, the only work James K. Vardaman thought these young black hands could perform.

The ethos of the blues is inescapable in the Delta, which my parents realized during the time they lived there. Some may associate the blues with the sinful music of the devil—James "Son" Thomas famously proclaimed, "the blues is nothing but the devil"—but for others the devil portrayed in the blues didn't have horns or bear a pitchfork; the devil was the white man who sought to control and dominate their lives. The white man as devil is the "big boss man" Jimmy Reed sings about who won't let him get a drink of water or the one who tells Big Bill Broonzy that "if you're black, get back." Of course, ideas about good and evil were racialized in a place that functioned on a strict racial binary like the Delta. Given the racially conscripted ways deemed available for self-expression, the literature—both written and in the music of the blues—was different for black and white residents.

The blues and the writing that came out of that system by African Americans in the Delta arose primarily out of resistance to the dominant culture. There was less focus for black Delta residents on a love of place and more on escaping from that place. Consequently the memoirs of black Delta life follow the classic pattern of the slave narrative: there is a loss of innocence, followed by a realization that there are alternatives to a life of bondage, then a decision to become free, and finally escape. That is what you see in Clifton Taulbert's memoir about growing up in the Delta town of Glen Allan, *When We Were Colored*. Taulbert found the inspiration to write this memoir when an aged relative passed along deeds that documented how his family once owned a sizeable tract of land—interestingly enough called Freemount—only to have it taken from them by crafty and greedy white people. After learning this, Taulbert realizes that in spite of the theft of his family's beloved property, they found strength in protecting and keeping themselves from further harm by following "the codes of growing up colored" in the Delta. The narrative arc follows Taulbert's learning of those codes, realizing there are other ways to live, and finally escaping from the Delta at the age of seventeen to pursue a college degree.

Endesha Ida Mae Holland grew up in the town of Greenwood without the connection to the land or the family support Taulbert grew to appreciate, yet the narrative patterns they use are similar. Where they differ is that Holland's work shows how even fewer options were available to black women. "In my Delta town, some black girls aspired to become the woman—the mistress of some wealthy white man. But the darker ones— like me—could make it by going to the cottonfields, working from sun to sun, for just about three dollars a day," Holland wrote in her play and subsequent memoir *From the Mississippi Delta*.

Holland's life was all about survival, which led her to become a prostitute at the age of twelve. One day, when seeking out a customer, she ended up following a young Student Nonviolent Coordinating Committee (SNCC) member to his office and in time became involved in the civil rights movement. Encouraged by the people she met in the movement, she found her way to college at the University of Minnesota, eventually earning a doctorate. *From the Mississippi Delta* focuses on the place that shaped her as much as how she found a way to escape from it.

Unlike Taulbert and Holland, William Attaway left his hometown of Greenville at a young age during the Great Migration of the black professional class who left the South. Born in 1911, Attaway was the son of a physician, and his family moved to Chicago when he was eleven. As a young man he worked with Richard Wright in the Federal Writers' Project and went on to write two novels: *Let Me Breathe Thunder* and *Blood on the Forge*. The latter is his best-known work and explores the fate of three African American brothers who during the Great Migration move north to Pennsylvania from a town in Kentucky that is every bit as violent as the Mississippi Delta it appears to be modeled on. "Jest as well I was born a nigger. Got more misery than a white man could stand," Attaway's character Big Mat proclaims to his brother, in a manner that would fit as well in Mississippi as in Kentucky and has the cadence of Delta blues.

Attaway may have left Mississippi at a young age, but the language of the brothers Big Mat, Melody, and Chinatown in *Blood on the Forge* is infused with the languorous rhythm of the blues, which undoubtedly migrated to Chicago alongside him. This novel stands as an example of how Mississippi's cultural impact flowed North and created an art form that has both endured and even become infused into the psyche of those who thought they had escaped it. The character Melody even laments his family's conditions in a song called "Hungry Blues":

> Done scratched at the hills,
> But the 'taters refuse to grow....
> Done scratched at the hills,
> But the 'taters refuse to grow....
> Mister Bossman, Mister Bossman,
> Lemme mark in the book one mo'....

A MADDENING BEAUTY

Although Attaway's writing is infused with the spirit of his native Delta, it's something a young writer named Ralph Ellison failed to see when he reviewed the novel. "Conceptually, Attaway grasped the destruction of the folk, but missed its rebirth at a higher level," Ellison said, indicating that he felt the novel focused too much on the destructive elements facing its characters rather than their redemption. After *Blood on the Forge*, Attaway never wrote another novel. He went on to write songs for Harry Belafonte—including the famous "Banana Boat Song"—as well as scripts for television and film, but he left fiction behind. Reading *Blood on the Forge* makes you wish Attaway had continued on a parallel path with his friend Richard Wright.

William Attaway and Richard Wright both found their literary voices in Chicago, a place like the Delta in that it is a flat landscape located under a beautiful searing sky and bordered by a large body of water. These men were among the thousands of black migrants from Mississippi who made the trip north to Chicago by taking the Illinois Central Railroad. This great demographic shift also led to what came to be known as the Black Chicago Renaissance, which began with the publication of Wright's *Uncle Tom's Children* in 1938. Wright set a pathway for a generation of African American fiction writers in Chicago that included, in addition to William Attaway, such figures as Arna Bontemps and Willard Motley, as well as poets like Gwendolyn Brooks.

Mississippi may have taken parts of its literature and the blues to Chicago, but it also brought the city a phrase that has become the name of its famous wind, one that turns up in blues songs about the city and reflects the culture of the Delta. Chicago's flat terrain may mirror the Mississippi Delta, only with a broad sky filled with tall buildings. Yet Lake Michigan, unlike the Mississippi River, stirs up a cold wind with a force that would only be found in the Delta during a tornado. African American migrants from Mississippi dubbed this almighty cold wind "the hawk," naming it for

Chicago was a destination for many African American migrants from Mississippi during the Great Migration, including Richard Wright, who was part of the Black Chicago Renaissance.

a bird they once observed flying over Delta fields at the same speed and with the same swiftness of movement. As Lou Rawls said in a 1967 performance during the monologue of his song "Dead End Street," "in Chicago, the Hawk not only socks it to you, he socks it through you, like a giant razor blade blowing down the street." Mississippi shares a strong cultural link to Chicago since those who fled the Magnolia State were refugees in their own country and sought to bring elements of the place they left behind with them as a comfort in the North. That is why it is appropriate that the northernmost marker on the Mississippi Blues Trail can be found near Grant Park in Chicago.

JUST AS THERE ARE MANY SOUTHS, there are many Deltas; the region's collective identity is often at odds with its various senses of itself, which are rooted in the people who live there and who left there, as well as the artists who have chosen to interpret them. There is the cotton kingdom

A cypress swamp in the Mississippi Delta.

Delta, the one from which all of its other narratives seem to flow, since without those fields of white gold the place as we know it today would not exist. As Jackson-based writer Gerard Helferich notes in *High Cotton*, "not only did cotton determine the history of the Delta and the South, it shaped the story of the nation." Then there is the Delta that is a primordial swath of Mississippi land, lingering under a seductive blanket of light, a source of poetic inspiration that shines, as Paul Simon says, like a National guitar and is also associated with the Delta of the blues. Of course, there is also the frontier Delta, an enclosed place that exists largely in the past yet is sometimes a layer through which the place is viewed.

As writer, critic, and observer of the American South Édouard Glissant noted in his work *Faulkner, Mississippi*, "Physical frontiers disappear more easily than mental ones, and for a frontier region such as the American South, it is hard to transcend the frontier. Today, there is a proliferation of frontier worlds, some traditional and others suddenly emergent, suggested to some and imposed on others." It is that desire to transcend the frontier that drives the literature of the Mississippi Delta. And sometimes out of that desire other worlds emerge, as can be found in the work of three Delta writers: Elizabeth Spencer, Lewis Nordan, and Steve Yarbrough. Each of these writers represented a new way of writing and thinking about the Delta as a literary setting, ways that evolved over the course of their three generations.

Although Elizabeth Spencer is best known for her novella set in Italy, *The Light in the Piazza*, her novel *The Voice at the Back Door* takes place in the fictional town of Lacey, a setting based on Spencer's hometown of Carrollton, which lies on the edge of the Delta. In the narrative of *The Voice at the Back Door* Spencer wrestles not so much with the physical landscape but with the landscape of memory, particularly when those past recollections are associated with violence. *The Voice at the Back Door*, published in 1956 during the post–Brown era, explores racial tensions surrounding life in Mississippi before the *Brown v. Board of Education* decision—the period of the novel's setting. This is a political novel and the very title of the book references the voices heard at the back door of many white homes: those of black servants. Race and memory also intersect as Spencer explores these ideas by taking an incident from her town's past—one she learned of during her childhood about a massacre of a dozen black men by a group of white men in the Carrollton courthouse in 1886—and examines how the reverberations of an incident from the Reconstruction era continue to have an impact on the people of her fictional town.

The real story of the courthouse massacre in Carrollton is one of tension and injustice, sparked when two black men charged a white man with attempted murder. On the day of the hearing for these charges, a number of black and white citizens were seated in the courtroom when a group of armed white men, said to number anywhere from fifty to one hundred, rode into town on horseback, dismounted at the courthouse, ran into the courtroom, and shot the plaintiffs, Ed and Charley Brown, and every other black person in the courtroom. No legal action was taken about the massacre, since the governor Robert Lowry commented in its aftermath, "The riot was provoked and perpetrated by the outrage and conduct of the Negroes."

The story of the Carrollton massacre was not one spoken about among its citizenry, silence being the preferred way of confronting difficult stories from the past. Yet the physical evidence of the massacre could be found in the bullet holes in the courthouse walls up until 1990, when they were covered during a renovation. Given this legacy of silence, Spencer chose to take this incident from the nineteenth century, place it in the early twentieth century, and use it to address issues of racial oppression in the town of Lacey as well as her own personal struggles with how race had cast a shadow on her Mississippi childhood. "I was under some sort of pressure within myself to clarify my own thinking about racial matters," Spencer recalled in an interview in 1989. "Many of my attitudes had been simply inherited, taken on good faith from those of good faith whom I loved. It seemed like blasphemy to question *them*, so I had to question myself. I could do that out of materials—incidents, people—which I already knew about. It was just in the melodramatic arrangement of the novel that I may have stepped things up a bit."

The Voice at the Back Door was Spencer's last book with a Mississippi setting, until her memoir, *Landscapes of the Heart*. In her memoir Spencer reveals how the publication of *The Voice at the Back Door* created a rift with her family, given that in the book she chose to expose the political structures of white supremacy and how it was undergirded by corruption and lawlessness. Even before the book was published, after a visit home to Carrollton, Spencer said she came to the conclusion, "I don't belong here anymore," since she knew that she questioned a system of apartheid that was masquerading as benevolence. Like many others before her, she took the train north out of Mississippi and left not only the place behind but also the very landscape that inspired her to become a writer.

It is common for Mississippi writers to experience alienation from the place they want to call home, yet how they confront that alienation and the cultural ecology of the state varies from writer to writer and evolves with each generation. Unlike Elizabeth Spencer, Lewis Nordan chose not to detach himself from Mississippi entirely. Shaped more by the post–World War II era than the Great Depression that was the backdrop of Spencer's life, Nordan could look at the Delta in another way rather than just removing himself from it. "The Mississippi Delta is not always dark with rain. Some autumn mornings the sun rises over Moon Lake, or Eagle, or Choctaw, or Blue, or Roebuck, all the wide, deep waters of the state, and when it does, its dawn is as rosy with promise and hope as any other."

Nordan decided to remake his Delta hometown of Itta Bena into a fictional place called Arrow Catcher, Mississippi, which serves as a bizarro

In his fiction, Lewis Nordan reimagined his hometown of Itta Bena as Arrow Catcher, Mississippi.

mirror image of Itta Bena. Unlike the real town, Arrow Catcher exists as a place of magical realism, one that blends the Southern idea of the grotesque and gothic with the magical and mysterious. In the process, Nordan finds that he can explore truths that exist on the Delta landscape in this fictional universe that he can't within the geographical confines of his hometown of Itta Bena.

Arrow Catcher may be a Delta town, but its geography exists outside the real world. The topography of the place changes from book to book, but there is one constant each time you enter this fictional world of Arrow Catcher, Mississippi: the place is populated by freaks. Whether it is in his books *The Sharpshooter Blues*, *Welcome to the Arrow Catcher Fair*, or *Music from the Swamp*, Nordan uses these freaks to recreate the Delta and its peculiar history. The book where Nordan does that best is *Wolf Whistle*, his reimagining of the torture and murder of fourteen-year-old Chicago native Emmett Till, who was lynched for allegedly whistling at a white

A MADDENING BEAUTY

woman while visiting relatives in Mississippi. What is most significant about *Wolf Whistle* is how race, place, and memory play a role in the narrative of the book. The way events surrounding the murder of Emmett Till have been remembered have been fraught from the beginning, something that is reflected in Nordan's framing and retelling of the story. Through his characters, the setting of Arrow Catcher, Mississippi, and his own memories of the Emmett Till murder, *Wolf Whistle* shows how social inequities, racial division, and self-loathing in the Delta led to the violence inflicted on Emmett Till.

The story of Emmett Till is one we think we all know, yet is one with many undiscovered edges and twists that have evolved over time. In the summer of 1955 a young African American boy from Chicago ventures into the Delta hamlet of Money and on a dare asks a white woman for "a date" and wolf whistles at her. He is then snatched away from the home of his relatives in the middle of the night and is beaten, tortured, and thrown in the Tallahatchie River anchored to an old cotton gin fan. Though his killers, store owner Roy Bryant and his half-brother J. W. Milam, were arrested and brought to trial less than a month after Till's body was found, the pair were acquitted by an all-white, all-male jury that deliberated for just sixty-seven minutes. Later, one juror said to a *Time* magazine reporter, "If we hadn't stopped to drink pop, it wouldn't have taken that long." This travesty of justice effectively made Till's murder a lynching.

While those facts seem both simple and chilling, the story is much more complicated, largely because of the way the accounts of Till's murder were distorted in a story written by journalist William Bradford Huie published in *LOOK* magazine in 1956. As scholar and writer Dave Tell has found in his research on Emmett Till and Southern memory, because one of the men featured in the *LOOK* story—Leslie Milam, a relative of the two men who committed the murder—did not enjoy the protections of double jeopardy, he did not sign a release form and he could not be mentioned in the story. Consequently the editors at *LOOK* moved the murder site 16.5 miles east to an abandoned spot of riverbank in Tallahatchie County. "The impact of that editorial decision on the landscape of the Mississippi Delta is difficult to exaggerate," Tell told me a few years ago. "Every map of Emmett Till's murder published between 1956 and 2005, between the *LOOK* account and the FBI report, left Sunflower County *off* the map entirely. To this day, Sunflower County is the only relevant county without a single built memorial to Till's murder."

It is perhaps because of this distortion of the landscape as it relates to Till's murder that it was a story Lewis Nordan saw could be moved to the town of Arrow Catcher and its fantastical Delta topography.

Emmett Till's murder haunted Lewis Nordan for much of his life. As he recounts in his memoir, *Boy with Loaded Gun*, he was so obsessed with the murder that he copied out in longhand every word that the *New York Times* had reported about the story in 1955. "I thought about it daily," Nordan recalled in his memoir. "I grieved it, but not with a social conscience, I'm sorry to say, and not with much compassion for Emmett Till or the loving

Bryant's Grocery in Money, Mississippi, now a weed-covered ruin, was at the center of the Emmett Till murder in 1955.

A MADDENING BEAUTY

mother who suffered his loss, but with a defensiveness that bordered on neurosis." The one thing Nordan could not admit to himself was that he felt culpable about what happened to Till, which is why he understands the darkness that might exist among some of his more unsavory characters. Rather than continuing his silence, he wrote *Wolf Whistle*.

In an essay at the end of *Wolf Whistle* Nordan describes the world of the novel as existing "on a plane, sometimes comic, even burlesque, just askew of the 'real,' historical universe." It's something the reader perceives in the overall flow of the narrative. The young school teacher Alice Conroy perceives Bobo's fate—Nordan uses Till's nickname instead of his real name—reflected in a magical drop of rain and later begins to see "children holding hands with grown-ups, black and white, singing 'We Shall Overcome.'" That same magical raindrop fades once Bobo dies, serving as a metaphor for the way the murder was repressed and not talked about for so long. A flock of buzzards, each named for a former governor of Mississippi—Vardaman, Bilbo, and Barnett—hover over the edge of town, as if they are waiting for the impending death by lynching. Alongside the buzzards there is a tamed hellhound that lives behind a bootleg whiskey store, a one-handed monkey named for the president of the Confederacy, and a parrot who cannot speak but can make the noise of a cash register. Bryant's Grocery, where the alleged fatal catcall was given, becomes Red's Goodlookin Bar and Gro. The character, Sugar Mecklin, serves as Nordan's alter ego in the narrative, and it is Sugar, along with his friend Sweet Austin, who finds Bobo's body. As the two boys stare at Bobo's mangled body, Nordan writes:

> In death, Bobo was patient. He had no care for quick identification. Soon enough, they would see the weight, they would see the wire, the bullet holes, the magic eye.

CHAPTER SEVEN

It is this "magic eye" that Alice Conroy has seen in the raindrop, foreshadowing this event. In this scene, by allowing Sugar to see the body and to lose his innocence, Nordan seems to be wishing that he had done the same; the connection perhaps might have allowed him to confront the events in a more direct and less tortured way. Once the magic eye fades, the town of Arrow Catcher has to reckon with the murder:

> There was much that Bobo still could have seen through the magical eye, but now Bobo had stopped seeing. This part was finished. Now Bobo was dead and gone.
> As so this was the day two white boys found a tattered corpse in the spillway waters of Roebuck Lake in Arrow Catcher, Mississippi.

Nordan moves the location of Bobo/Till's body to a lake near his hometown, one that is a part of his fictional landscape and is separate from the spot along the Tallahatchie River where Till's body was actually found. "This is the white story of the murder of Emmett Till," Nordan said in an interview with *The Southern Quarterly* in 2003, a decade after the release of *Wolf Whistle*, meaning the book was a means of confronting the guilt and silence of white Delta residents about the murder as well as the social tension and rules of white supremacy that led to the murder. But the story Nordan tells is also one of how Till's death left an indelible mark on the Delta terrain, one we have seen echoed in the present, as the commemorative marker by the Tallahatchie River where Till's body was found has been vandalized again and again. In Nordan's world, Bobo/Till's death is an event no one can avoid or erase from memory, not even two innocent young boys who happen to come across a dead body. That remains true today on the real landscape of the Delta.

If Lewis Nordan sought to remake the Delta landscape as a Southern land of magical realism in his fiction, Steve Yarbrough chose to confront the real consequences the geography of the Delta inflicts on its

A MADDENING BEAUTY

ABOVE The setting of Lewis Nordan's *Wolf Whistle* was inspired by this streetscape in his hometown of Itta Bena.
BELOW Nordan moved the location of Bobo/Till's body from the Tallahatchie River to this lake near his hometown.

residents through his characters. As a writer shaped by the civil rights era in Mississippi, Yarbrough feels less confined by the old ways in which a white writer from the Delta could write about the region. In his lifetime he has witnessed the land move from a place defined by Jim Crow and sharecropper shacks to post civil rights movements marked by an ascendant black political class; yet the Delta remains a place controlled by the interest of white landowners. "I find the region limitless," Yarbrough told the *Arkansas Review* in 2002. "I could tell any story I wanted and set it there."

Yarbrough has used the fictional Delta town of Loring, Mississippi, as the setting for four of his novels: *Visible Spirits*, *Prisoners of War*, *The End of California*, and *Safe from the Neighbors*. In these four novels Yarbrough explores what the Delta's past can tell us about the present, whether it is the impact of racism on the life of a black postmistress in Loring in 1902 (*Visible Spirits*) or the reverberations of the Ole Miss riot on a history teacher in the same town in the early 2000s (*Safe From the Neighbors*) or how German prisoners of war—who worked on Delta plantations during World War II—left their mark on the Delta (*Prisoners of War*). But it is his first novel, *The Oxygen Man*, that focuses on the impact the geography of the Delta has on the men and women who call it home.

As the cotton industry went into decline, many cotton fields were plowed over and then catfish ponds were dug, and these ponds began to frame the Delta landscape with glistening water that sometimes even attracted migratory birds. From the 1970s through the mid-1990s farm-raised catfish was sold to farmers as the next crop that would keep the Delta as prosperous as the days when it was the cotton kingdom. The oxygen man in the book's title is Ned Rose, and he is responsible for ensuring that the catfish ponds are aerated properly and that the crop is safe. The action that sets the novel in motion happens when, as an act of protest for inequities in the workplace, a group of black workers cut a diesel line and

A MADDENING BEAUTY

spoil fifty thousand dollars' worth of fish. The conflicts that result play out on an altered physical landscape and focus on the shifting geography of race. And because of the groundwork laid by writers like Elizabeth Spencer and Lewis Nordan, Yarbrough has the freedom to explore these issues in a more pointed and direct way.

The presence of water on the landscape is the great metaphor of *The Oxygen Man*, serving as a reminder to readers that the landscape of the Delta has been remade over and over by the impact of water, whether it was from the centuries of flooding that created the alluvial plain the land rests upon or by the Great Flood of 1927. "By rights, water ought to be all over the Delta," one character observes. "You know there wasn't much solid land here a hundred years ago?" Catfish ponds are just another physical intervention on the land of the Delta, yet one that is both familiar and frightening. But not only is the land of the Delta being changed,

The proliferation of commercial catfish ponds in the Delta—aerated by machines like these beside their banks—became another physical intervention on the region's landscape.

CHAPTER SEVEN

the people who inhabit the land are changing. By focusing on a dispute with black workers over workplace injustice—an action that could not have occurred before the civil rights movement—Yarbrough seeks to show how while the land may look different with vast shimmering ponds of catfish rather than cotton, the same injustices that were part of the old farming system are a part of the new one. They have just been passed down to the next generation.

The narrative of *The Oxygen Man* takes place largely in 1996, the peak of the Delta catfish industry, but also flashes back to its origins in the 1970s. It is also set in Yarbrough's native Sunflower County and the town of Indianola where he grew up, which makes the action that occurs on the landscape feel more like documentary evidence collected by the author and less like fiction. In addition to the geography of the land, Yarbrough examines how race and class exist on the landscape, whether it is by mentioning the segregation academy (a colloquial term for private schools) Ned attended—as Yarbrough himself did as well—or how class determines where people sit at a football game.

In the fiction of Steve Yarbrough there are signs of how the civil rights era liberated Mississippi writers, allowing them to see not only the landscape in a different way but also how injustice is manifested on the great expanse of land known as the Delta. Across his novels his characters in some way all confront an injustice that is inherent in the Delta. There are also signs of how Yarbrough has learned from others who have tackled writing about the land, whether it is Elizabeth Spencer or Lewis Nordan or even William Alexander Percy. "We all learn through imitation," he says. "And the more sources you're drawing from, I think the more likely you are to come up with something that's not quite like anything else. I think ultimately, there are only so many stories to tell, but there are any number of different voices."

A MADDENING BEAUTY

"*The Mississippi Delta* will be the last place on earth to be paved over," Willie Morris penned in a neat cursive hand on his edits to the conclusion of an essay for the Mississippi Forestry Experiment Station in 1989. While it seems an unlikely place to find an essay by Morris, for anyone who wants to understand the Delta in the post–World War II era, his writing is a touchstone. His widow, JoAnne, shared the essay with me, which interestingly enough he continued to revise even after it had been published. There is a beauty and a rhythm to the finished piece but the additions added another layer of polish. "Willie was always revising," JoAnne told me one afternoon, "whether it was on the page or in his head."

What comes through in Willie Morris's writing is his love of his native Delta, a place he said he knew better than his own heart. In writing about his native Yazoo City, he acknowledges that in his youth the place was "not in our souls then,

CHAPTER SEVEN

Willie Morris's return to Mississippi and the roads of his native Delta like this
one gave him a new perspective on the place he called home.

only in our pores, as familiar to me as water or grass or sunlight." Yazoo City marks the beginning of the Delta. During Willie's youth, as well as my own, a driver who headed northward on the two-lane U.S. 49 would enter the town with what felt like a sudden and precipitous drop down a hill, into a place that was lush, green, and flat. When you come from a part of Mississippi where you move from hills to flat land so dramatically, it's a perfect setting in which to become a writer because you're from a place that feels like both a beginning *and* an ending. That is why the Delta seeped into Morris's very being from the very beginning.

William Weaks Morris may have returned to the university town of Oxford after his days in the New York literary world, but he never lost his connection to the land that he believed made him a writer. No one else except Willie—and everyone called him Willie—could say about the Delta, "It is still Old Testament to me in its ageless rhythms and despairs." For Willie, the Delta was a place of spiritual communion and scripture that was to be interpreted and debated. It was also where he confronted both his personal ghosts as well as those that haunt the entire state of Mississippi. Although Morris is best known as a Southern storyteller, what Willie Morris did—whether it was about sports and race in *The Courting of Marcus Dupree*, his childhood dog in *My Dog Skip*, or his novel as memoir *Taps*—was change the way people in Mississippi and those outside of it thought about the Delta as a place, visually and culturally. Willie changed the way we see the Delta.

There is a romantic notion of the Delta that Willie inherited from other writers before him such as William Alexander Percy and David Cohn. But after he pulls you into the romance of the land that shaped him, just as those other writers do, he exposes the social structure that lies just beneath the surface. Yazoo City may have been a pleasant town to grow up in for a white boy in the 1940s, with its streets "swooping out of the hills" as he writes in *North Toward Home*. But it was also the same town where the black doctor who saved his life when he was a year old had to enter the back door of the house to treat him. There may have been beauty in the Yazoo City of Willie's youth, but he is also telling his reader that this same land—poor old beat-down Mississippi, as he called it—was shaped on certain traditions, not all of them ones to be proud of. Willie wanted his readers to see both of those Deltas. Yet in order to change the way we gaze upon Mississippi's expansive and flat alluvial plain, first Willie had to leave it.

Leaving home in order to find it is the core of Willie's memoir *North Toward Home*, which is as much about his political and intellectual formation as it is about his connection to the place where he was born and raised. At the center of how Willie became a writer is his connection to and rejection of a place that valued social conformity, while he sought a way to explore the world beyond the borders of the place he called home. Willie found an interest and curiosity in something beyond what he called "my own parochial ego" at the University of Texas. When he arrived in Austin in the fall of 1952 on a Southern Trailways bus, he remembered hearing the words of a popular song at the time that let him know that although he was departing from his beloved Delta, he still belonged to the place he was leaving behind:

> Fly the ocean in a silver plane
> See the jungle when it's wet with rain
> Just remember 'til you're home again
> You belong to me.

In his years at the University of Texas, as a Rhodes Scholar at Oxford University, and as a magazine editor and writer in New York, Willie Morris never lost the connection to his native Delta and Yazoo City. He also never stopped questioning the role that racial politics played in his native land. These impulses create a unique push and pull familiar to any Mississippian who has lived in the North as a Southern expatriate. "Why

231

A MADDENING BEAUTY

was it, in such moments just before I leave the South, did I always feel some easing of a great burden?" he wrote in the opening of the last paragraph of *North Toward Home*. It's something I have wrestled with, as someone who divides his life between the North and the South, feeling at home in both places but also feeling my unbreakable connection with Mississippi both a joy and a tremendous psychic weight.

Willie Morris taught Mississippians that they can love the Magnolia State and still be critical of it, and that criticism is a way of showing your love of the land of your birth. No, Willie did not hate Mississippi. He loved it, but hated certain things about it and wanted them to change. It's almost as if he took the lessons he learned from attending Sunday school at the First United Methodist Church in Yazoo City and combined them with his reading of Saint Augustine from his philosophy classes at the University of Texas. Those two experiences seem to have created in him an idea about his relationship with Mississippi: love the place, hate its sins, and find ways of atoning for those sins. Willie's means of atonement was his writing.

Former Mississippi governor William Winter became a close friend of Willie Morris's, a bond that was formed when the two men participated in a panel discussion at Millsaps College in 1981, along with Willie's friend and novelist William Styron. The discussion examined the rich literary tradition of Mississippi and how the "burdens" of Southern history had contributed to the flowering of this culture. During the event, Willie wrote a note to himself: "He [Winter] is saying things which no Governor of a Deep Southern state has ever said, and with the eloquence of a Stevenson or a John Kennedy. This is a historic moment for Mississippi." Because of the connection between the two men, eighteen years later, after Willie Morris's sudden death at age sixty-five, William Winter wanted to find a way to honor his friend, who had also shared his interest in racial reconciliation. As a trustee of the Mississippi Department of Archives and History, Governor Winter arranged for Willie's body to lie in state in the

Old Capitol Museum in Jackson, the same building where Mississippi had seceded from the Union. He was the first writer and only the third person in that century to be given that honor. His friend Pat Conroy, upon hearing that Willie's body was to lie in state in the Old Capitol, told Rick Bragg of the *New York Times*, "The State of Mississippi knows how to treat a writer."

Because Willie Morris became an outsider, while still maintaining his insider identity as a Mississippian, he opened up part of Mississippi to the rest of the world. Because he tried to lift the veil off the mystery of the Delta, I believe that is why it is not unheard of for writers from outside the region to want to see the Delta as a setting for their own work. The most successful works are by writers who follow a pattern that is the reverse of the one Willie chose: they seek to become insiders while at the same time keeping their status as outsiders.

Although he does not feel the influence of Willie Morris, British travel writer Richard Grant made the Delta town of Pluto his home and told the story of his time there in what is one of the best contemporary examinations of the culture of the Mississippi Delta, *Dispatches from Pluto: Lost and Found in the Mississippi Delta*. Grant has lived all around the world, yet his attraction to the Delta is the same as Willie Morris's. "It was the setting that attracted me," Grant remarked. "Big sky, golden light, cotton fields and cypress swamps, birds everywhere, deer in the woods." Although he now calls Mississippi home, in the tradition of Willie Morris, Grant clings to his outsider status. "I'm not really from anywhere," Grant said in an interview with *South Writ Large* in 2016. "I was born in Malaysia, lived in Kuwait as a boy, then London. I've lived in twenty different houses on four different continents. I'm rootless and have no strong conception of home," unlike Mississippi-born writers.

But that doesn't mean that he doesn't understand the Delta. Grant's rootlessness serves him well in seeing both the beauty and the troubles of the Delta as well as the assorted characters that dot the landscape, such as catfish farmers, blues singers, and eccentric rich white people. As he wrote in *Dispatches from Pluto*, "Lyndon Johnson said, 'there's America, there's the South, and then there's Mississippi.'" His friend, Mississippi-born food writer Martha Foose, stopped him and interjected, "And then there's the Delta. You have no idea of what you are getting into down here, and that's what makes it so perfect." Grant looks at the Delta landscape as more a part of the global south (typically areas outside of the United States and Europe that are low or middle income) and not just part of the geographical South, which adds a layer of complexity to his perspective.

When Georgia native Cynthia Shearer decided to set her second novel, *The Celestial Jukebox*, in the Delta, she wasn't necessarily thinking about focusing her narrative around the idea of the global south, but it just happened to fall in her lap. Her main character, Boubacar, a fifteen-year-old refugee from Mauritania, came to her after a conversation she had with the first U.S. immigration judge to be posted in Memphis, who happened to be visiting William Faulkner's Rowan Oak in 1998 when Shearer was the curator there. "We talked a long time about Mauritanians coming from a place where slavery was still legal, to work in the casinos at Tunica." That got her thinking about how the Delta would look to someone from what we now call the Global South and how that perspective would shape the way they connected with the landscape. "I ended up doing what I would call documentary fiction and straight-up ethnography, rather than reading literary treatments of it for comparison," Shearer told me. In writing about the Delta, Shearer also brought insights from the culture of her native south Georgia, a place that is also covered by the shadow of a sharecropping legacy. Although the agrarian aspect of her setting was familiar, she wanted to look at the Delta from a fresh perspective. "I was interested in documenting the new ethnicities arriving in the Delta, which I saw as hopeful. And I was interested in privileging the 'outsider' African perspective over the white perspective in the novel, because that had not been done before."

234

Willie Morris's grave in Glenwood Cemetery, which includes these words he wrote: "Even across the divide of death, friendship remains an echo forever in the heart."

The idea of privileging the outsider is what connects Richard Grant and Cynthia Shearer with the work of Willie Morris. For a man who had what he called a parochial ego, Morris always sought out a wider context to view the place he loved. Through his writing, he sought to find a way for Mississippians—and all Americans—to look through the fog that covers the way we see the terrain of the Delta and gain a sense of cultural and moral clarity.

In the Yazoo City of today it can be difficult to imagine the bucolic small town of Willie Morris's childhood, one free of the commercial sprawl that now spreads like kudzu out on U.S. Route 49 with its fast food spots, Dollar General stores, and prisons, both state and federal. To find the world Willie knew, you must enter the gates of Glenwood Cemetery where he is buried. It is there you can find the witch's grave he mentions in *Good Old Boy* and you can see where he played taps as soldiers were buried during the Korean War. It is in Glenwood Cemetery near Willie's grave in the silence that envelops that spot that you can also hear Morris's alter ego Swayze in his novel *Taps* saying, "An echo, I would learn, was a kind of life in perpetuity, remote and immune, distant lingering notes from afar, sweetly voyeuristic, while the grave was, after all, the grave."

Mississippi's literature from the Delta region reveals that there are countless ways of looking at this land and hearing the distant lingering notes it sings to those who come to it for inspiration. Novelist Richard Ford is one such writer. He wrote *The Sportswriter*—a novel set in New Jersey—in the reading room of the Carnegie Public Library in Clarksdale. "The Delta is where I chose to live," Ford said. "The Carnegie Library is a refuge." Ford now has a marker on the Mississippi Literary Heritage Trail in Clarksdale rather than marking his birthplace in Jackson. When asked why he chose Clarksdale and the Carnegie Library, Ford said, "They offered me a haven. I want to be remembered in a place where people could go read books. Literature can be a way for society to address what it doesn't want to address."

Literature can also serve as a means of focusing on cultural change, both socially and on the landscape. There is a feeling among Mississippians that the Delta is a landscape that is unchanging, when in fact it is one that has been evolving for centuries, just like the river that hugs the western boundary of this region. And it continues to evolve, much like the writers who have chosen to write about it.

Given the vastness of the land, as Willie Morris once wrote, "the Mississippi Delta will be the last place on earth to be paved over."

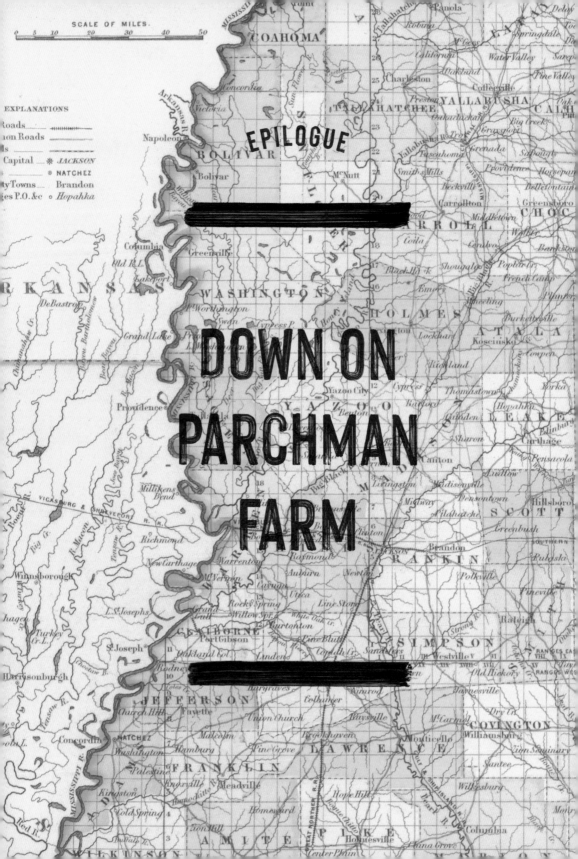

EPILOGUE

DOWN ON PARCHMAN FARM

I died in Korea from a shrapnel wound, and
narcotics rescued me. I died in 1960 from a prison
sentence and poetry brought me back to life.

—Etheridge Knight

W HEN CORINTH NATIVE Etheridge Knight dropped out of school
at sixteen to join the Army, he had no intentions of becoming a
poet. The military was simply a means of escape from the impoverished
circumstances of his upbringing. When he entered the army in 1947, he
scored so high on intelligence tests that his supervisors at Fort Knox questioned his results. His superiors reexamined him, yet failed in their search
for signs of his having cheated. After suffering wounds in Korea, he found
refuge in morphine from the physical and emotional pain he felt in the
aftermath of war. It wasn't long before Knight was hooked on opioids.

Like many addicts, his illicit habit led to a life of crime, which for
Knight eventually landed him in an Indiana prison. His charge: he and
two associates "unlawfully, feloniously, forcibly by violence" tried to rob
a woman of ten dollars. This was a crime the justice system deemed wor-
thy of his serving a 10- to 25-year sentence so "the best interest of society
could be served."

In the best interest of society, Knight discovered literature. While in
prison, Knight began to read voraciously, emerged as a letter writer for
other inmates—who lined up for his services—and became a journalist
for prison publications. Though he did not realize it, his experiences after
dropping out of school in pool halls, juke joints, and poker games served as
the foundation to his becoming a poet and writer; it was in those spaces he
gained an agility with language. His education in prison through reading

PARCHMAN FARM BLUES

The Mississippi State Penitentiary at Parchman has inspired many songs, including "Parchman Farm Blues" by singer-guitarist Booker "Bukka" White, who was once an inmate here, and "Parchman Farm" by jazz singer-pianist Mose Allison. Folklorists from the Library of Congress and other institutions also came to Parchman beginning in the 1930s to document the pre-blues musical forms of field hollers and work songs, which survived here due to the prison's relative isolation from modern cultural influences.

The gates outside the Mississippi State Penitentiary at Parchman.

led to an apprenticeship as a writer, attracting notice inside the prison walls as well as outside of them. He eventually gained the attention of renowned Chicago poet Gwendolyn Brooks, who began guiding his work with the firm critiques she was famous for issuing to young black poets.

What Knight did was take the aesthetic of black vernacular speech and transform it through utterance and performance into poetry. "There ain't no universal aesthetics. It's impossible," he told the critic Sanford Pinsker in 1983. "Therefore, *any* aesthetic, to me, has to be subjective, personal, within a group." His poems are all personal but in one way or another all come back to his roots in Mississippi, like "A Poem for Myself (or Blues for a Mississippi Black Boy)":

> I'm still the same old black boy with the same old blues.
>
> Going back to Mississippi
>
> This time to stay for good
>
> Going back to Mississippi
>
> This time to stay for good—
>
> Gonna be free in Mississippi
>
> Or dead in the Mississippi mud.

Etheridge Knight's aesthetic as a poet was shaped by Mississippi as much as it was by his time in prison in Indiana. As Knight once wrote, "It is hard / To make a poem in prison. / The air lends itself not / to the singer." But somehow Knight persevered with his art, using poetic strength as a weapon against the annihilation of the sprit that takes place within a prison's walls. Knight's body of work made me wonder whether there were men and women like him inside Mississippi's prisons today, finding refuge in poetry and writing. Mississippi, the poorest state in the union, has twenty-one prisons—both public and private—and in the Delta, the poorest region of the state, the prison system is a major employer. Sometimes it seems as if the choice in the Delta for a young person is to find a way to leave—perhaps by entering the military as Knight did or, if they are lucky, by going to college—or if they stay to work in the prison system or end up in the prison system itself.

Complicating today's Mississippi Delta is access to education, which continues to be a civil rights issue in this part of the state. School is no longer delayed for cotton picking season as it was when the crop required physical labor, but there is barely enough money to keep schools up and running. In 2017, the Mississippi Supreme Court ruled that the legislature is not obliged to fully fund schools in the state, a ruling that hits poor districts in Delta towns with a wallop. Consequently, education has not become the great equalizer for opportunity in the Delta many hoped it would become after the end of segregation.

On my trips up and down through the Delta, I often drive past the Mississippi State Penitentiary, the notorious Parchman Farm that Booker "Bukka" White sings of in "Parchman Farm Blues." Sometimes I can hear him singing these words:

> I'm down on Parchman farm
> I sho' wanna go back home
> I'm down on Parchman farm
> But I sho' wanna go back home
> But I hope some day
> I will overcome

Parchman casts a long shadow in this country's creative imagination, having served as the inspiration for the prison farm in the films *Cool Hand Luke* and *O Brother, Where Art Thou?* In Mississippi's literary imagination, Parchman finds its way into both the blues music and literature of the state, touching every corner of the state's cultural landscape. It is referred to as an unescapable "destination doom" in William Faulkner's *The Mansion*. By having her character Jack Renfro in her novel *Losing Battles* return from

Parchman, Eudora Welty lets you know why when he returns to the scarcity and want of his hometown of Banner he can only perceive the place of his birth as peaceful and luxurious. The characters in Jesmyn Ward's *Sing, Unburied, Sing* reveal the real and psychic costs of cycles of trauma, poverty, and violence designed to siphon vulnerable people into jails and prisons like Parchman. It was Ward's character Michael who put it best, writing of Parchman in a letter to his wife, Leonie, "This ain't no place for no man. Black or White. Don't make no difference. This is a place for the dead."

Prisoners once hoed the vast cotton fields of Parchman's twenty thousand acres.

In her biography *Trials of the Earth*, Mary Hamilton wrote, "I know I am the first white woman that ever came through what is now Parchman." Hamilton and her husband were there when the land was cleared. Once the land was cleared, a penal farm was established at the direction of Governor James K. Vardaman, who saw Parchman as a means of dealing with "criminal negroes." Parchman was established by eliciting racial fear and was unique among American prisons because of its financial profitability: the land was a profit-driven farm that was once the state's largest source of revenue outside of income taxes.

While I was growing up in Mississippi in the 1960s and 1970s, there was no other prison in the state, making the place synonymous with crime, punishment, and brutality. If you went to prison, you went to Parchman. It was common knowledge that a trip to Parchman was not just to pay for a crime. The purpose of the sentence at Parchman Farm was also to humiliate and break the spirit of those who pushed against the status quo in the state. It was Parchman, in a section of the prison known as "little Alcatraz," where the state of Mississippi placed the Freedom Riders in 1961 and later other civil rights protestors for "breach of peace." Several years later in 1970, it was also at Parchman where an overflow of nearly forty African American students from the University of Mississippi were placed after taking part in a protest to call attention to a list of black student demands. Humiliation has always been part of the punishment at Parchman. Its remote, nearly treeless location of twenty-eight square miles in the middle of the Delta equates its very name with punishment of a violent, vindictive variety. Today there is also a privately run prison in the Delta, in addition to other regional "detention facilities" that seem to pop up across the state. But Parchman's twenty thousand acres command an outsized presence, both in the Delta and in Mississippi. The expansive network of fences, razor wire, and guard towers that keep its prisoners tightly inside Parchman's borders make this flat expanse of land feel like a large gaping wound on the landscape.

Mississippi's black writers traditionally have left the region to hone their craft or to find an environment that will allow them to explore their art. Had Etheridge Knight landed in prison in Mississippi in the 1960s and 1970s, it is unlikely that he would have found his poetic voice. In Mississippi, Parchman was a place meant exclusively for punishment; it was not a place for an education, self-directed or otherwise. Mississippi became a motif in Knight's work, but he had to be imprisoned above the Mason-Dixon Line in Indiana to find his linkage to the place of his birth.

Today the Delta can be a difficult place for a poor black person to escape. "Poverty travels with an entourage," wrote Parchman inmate Gregory Frazier in his memoir essay "Snake Creek." According to Frazier, the members of that entourage include "tragedy, crime, shame, pain, and death. All of which I have gotten to know on a first-name basis." Based on my reading of essays and poetry published over the past five years from classes at Parchman, run by writer Louis E. Bourgeois, I had begun to wonder whether there might be another generation of writers like Etheridge Knight who are in prisons across the state. Bourgeois runs a nonprofit, Mississippi Prison Writes, one that provides a network of classes on writing and literature in several facilities in the state prison system. On a chilly fall morning I decided to visit his class at Parchman in a room surrounded by surveillance cameras and filled with six men eager to read, write, and discuss literature.

The members of Louis Bourgeois's writing and literature class at Parchman study writers from Camus to Kierkegaard, from Richard Wright to William Faulkner. And they pursue their studies in a setting that seems at odds with the pursuit of learning and knowledge. The morning I traveled there, a bruise-colored sky hung firmly over the vast fields surrounding Parchman, with a fine cold mist falling from the dark blue–streaked clouds.

To enter the black steel gates I show my identification and gaze back and watch the bars close together with a slide and a clang, imagining what it would be like to not know when they would open again. Parchman was built in 1901 and Louis and I enter one of the original buildings for the class. Soon after signing in—and making sure we are free of any contraband like mobile phones and cigarettes—six prisoners are gathered together. Soon we learn that one member has been transferred to another unit and will no longer be able to be a part of the class. On this day we are discussing prison narratives, specifically *De Profundis* ("From the Depths"), written by Oscar Wilde during his imprisonment for "gross indecency," as well as a contemporary prison narrative. Both texts are analyzed through the critical perspective of French philosopher Michel Foucault's *Discipline and Punish: The Birth of the Prison*, which examines how prisons have shifted the focus of punishment from the body to the soul. One student sees parallels between Foucault and George Jackson's *Blood in My Eye*. Take away the surveillance cameras and prison stripes, and the discussion could be one taking place in any college classroom. Yet the video cameras hovering over the room remind me that in prison one is under perpetual surveillance. With the loss of freedom comes a loss of privacy, and you feel that imposed exposure intensely within an instant of stepping inside Parchman.

The men are evenly split between black and white and the discussion moves from the two prison narratives to how the writers' words mirror their life inside Parchman. This is not a high-security section of the prison, yet one of the readings, the students remind me, provides a window into what they would describe as "the red zone," a place with a risk for violence. There is a line in the reading that all respond to positively: "You will never be the master if you never kill your idols." In other words, everyone needs to know how to decipher the truth. For these men, I come to understand that possessing the means to decoding what is true and meaningful is essential to their survival.

DOWN ON PARCHMAN FARM

This once-a-week class provides a means of thought-provoking conversation for these men that nourishes them for the remainder of the week. "This class keeps my mind engaged in a way that allows me to feel as if my life is worthwhile. I worry that other men here don't have this or can't imagine doing this." This is a man who, like Etheridge Knight, writes letters for other prisoners, some of whom are barely literate. I begin to tell them all about the life and poetry of Etheridge Knight and they ask me to come back for a lecture and discussion of his work. Louis sees this as a way for the men to begin to think about writing their own poems about prison and selects a group of poems that he feels will connect with the men's experiences.

There are no women at Parchman today, Bourgeois reminds me, although there was a section for women until 1986. Up until then, the women even had their own section of land to farm. Bourgeois's Prison Writes Initiative conducts classes with women at the Central Mississippi Correctional Facility in Pearl very much like the one structured for the men: the focus is philosophy, literature, and writing. The common connection between the writing of the women and the men is often the experience of poverty. Yet a theme that turns up more often for the women is abuse. "From as long as I could remember, my home life was violent," wrote Linda Ross. "A peaceful home was being molested in one way or another."

Before we leave Parchman that day, Louis drives me around parts of the expansive grounds of the prison, which stretches across five miles from east to west. We visit the cemetery, which I expected to be full beyond capacity of men and women who died within these walls, but it has an entire empty section. Off in the distance, we can see Unit 29 of the prison, which is the maximum-security facility and also has writing classes. I'm reminded of how John Grisham took his readers inside that part of Parchman—otherwise known as "death row"— in *The Chamber*, a narrative that makes a strong statement against capital punishment. I begin to wonder how many of the white crosses were executed by the state and how many lives just faded behind these walls, unclaimed by families and buried here.

WHEN I PASS THROUGH the gates of Parchman two weeks later, the men are eager to take part in the discussion of Etheridge Knight. They have all read his work and are ready to begin as soon as we enter the door. I feel self-consciously professorial, particularly when one of the men admires the fresh shine on my loafers and my brightly striped socks. Quickly I turn the conversation from the dress that sets me apart from the men inside these prison walls to the poetry of Etheridge Knight, pointing out the rhythm and musicality of Knight's writing and the influence of the blues in its cadences. The topics of loss, love, and oppression in the poems we read connect with the men, reminding me that in spite of the passage of time since Knight wrote his poetry, little has changed in prisons in either America or Mississippi, with the exception of the number of people incarcerated. Since Knight published *Born of a Woman* in 1980, Mississippi's prison population has risen by 392 percent. When we read a poem from that collection, "Hard Rock Returns to Prison from the Hospital for the Criminal Insane," the men all agree that they have all known someone like the central figure of the poem, Hard Rock, a man who had the scars to prove his toughness and resiliency behind bars. For his toughness he is lobotomized, "his eyes empty like knot holes in a fence," reminding the men that one way or another—medically, physically, or spiritually—the prison system finds a way to tame you.

The men responded to the visceral pain and loss Knight reflects on in "Feeling Fucked Up" or the sadness and reflection on addiction in "The Idea of Ancestry." In "For Freckle Faced Gerald," an elegy for the lost innocence of a boy raped in prison, Knight's use of rhyme, metaphor, and allusion renders the poem as addressing larger issues of oppression inside prison as well as sexual violence:

> Take Gerald. Sixteen years hadn't even done
> a good job on his voice. He didn't even know
> how to talk tough, or how to hide the glow
> of life before he was thrown in as "pigmeat"
> for the buzzards to eat.

Next we turn to the final poem for our discussion, "A WASP Woman Visits a Black Junkie in Prison." One man focuses on these lines:

> After the seating
> And the greeting, they fished for a denominator,
> Common or uncommon;
> And could only summon up the fact that both were human.

While I tried to capture the tone and texture of Knight's poetry when I read his words, I remind the students that Knight was "a poet of the belly," meaning he was a man who could expose the emotions he felt deep inside his guts with the inflections of his voice. My focus when teaching poetry is language, making me realize I had emphasized Knight's wordplay, as a scholar would, more than his raw emotion. The men focused on the unvarnished feelings Knight forces on the page, because they can connect with the words in a way I never can in my speech and delivery of his poems, no matter how hard I try. I might be able to place Etheridge Knight within the literary lineage of Mississippi and the Delta, but only the men in this class inside these prison walls knew how Knight's words reflected the emotional regions of their lives.

As we wrap up the class, the men ask me if I will come again. Of course, I say, yes, thinking of Knight's WASP woman, searching for a common or uncommon denominator. But unlike Knight's poetic subject, I feel a connection here, more common than uncommon. No longer will I drive along U.S. Route 49 past the walls of Parchman and wonder about the lives of the souls kept inside its vast fields bordered by concrete walls, barbed wire, and electrified gates that clang tightly shut. When I drive by Parchman—or any other prison in Mississippi or America, for that matter—I will not think merely of the punishment that takes place inside and the crimes that placed the people there. I will think of the inner lives of the men and women in prisons who are seeking redemption through writing, struggling each time they put pen to paper to capture their lives in both poetry and prose.

And I will think of their stories, which are Mississippi's stories. These men I have encountered inside Parchman's walls are my fellow Mississippi writers.

Highway 49 north, just outside Parchman's gates. Parchman casts a long
shadow in America's and Mississippi's creative imaginations.

NOTES

CHAPTER ONE

"black soldiers, and Ship Island." —Page 31, Charles Henry Rowell, "Inscriptive Restorations: An Interview with Natasha Trethewey," *Callaloo* 27, no. 4 (Fall 2004).

"It remembers without diminishing." —Page 31, "Necessary Utterance: On Poetry As a Cultural Force," *The Virginia Quarterly Review* 90, no. 1 (2014). https://www.vqronline.org/ necessary-utterance.

CHAPTER FOUR

"our behavior but how to feel." —Page 104, Eudora Welty, "Must the Novelist Crusade?" in *The Eye of the Story: Selected Essays and Reviews* (New York: Penguin Random House), p. 154.

CHAPTER SIX

"a bare room smelling of stale tobacco." —Page 159, Thomas S. Hines, *William Faulkner and the Tangible Past : The Architecture of Yoknapatawpha* (University of California Press, 1996).

one year before its publication. —Page 165, J. H. Justus, "Enduring Modernism: Stark Young and the Nashville Agrarians," *Southern Review* 39, no. 2 (2003); p 419.

CHAPTER SEVEN

his unextravagant hills. —Page 187, Willie Morris, "My Delta. And Yours?" in *A Social and Economic Portrait of the Mississippi Delta*, edited by Arthur G. Cosby, Mitchell W. Brackin, T. David Mason, and Eunice R. McCulloch (Social Science Research Service, Mississippi State University, 1992).

From France for a single room in his house. —Page 192, James C. Cobb, *The Most Southern Place on Earth: The Mississippi Delta and the Roots of Regional Identity* (New York: Oxford University Press, 1992), p. 18.

"wealth and prosperity culminate." —Page 194, Cobb, *The Most Southern Place on Earth*, p. 28.

Hill-billy towns. —Page 197, Charles G. Bell, "The Hills" in *Delta Return* (Bloomington: Indiana University Press, 1956).

"right man in the wrong place." —Page 201, William Alexander Percy Diary, William Alexander Percy Papers, Mississippi Department of Archives and History, Jackson, Mississippi, October 17, 1910.

"could do here [in the Delta]." —Page 201, William Alexander Percy Diary, William Alexander Percy Papers, Mississippi Department of Archives and History, Jackson, Mississippi, October 17, 1910.

"and know it's true."—Page 206, Betty Tardieu, "'I'm in That Secular World, Even Though I Keep Looking Around for Someplace Else To Be': Interview with Ellen Douglas," *Southern Quarterly* 33, no. 4 (1995).

"memorial to Till's murder."—Page 221, "For Better or Worse, How Mississippi Remembers Emmett Till: W. Ralph Eubanks and Dave Tell on the Legacy of a Murder," *Literary Hub*, November 2, 2016. https://lithub.com/for-better-or-worse-how-mississippi-remembers-emmett-till/.

"any number of different voices."—Page 227, Hillary Casavant, "Steve Yarbrough: Can't Stop Telling," *The Writer*, October 21, 2018. https:// www.writermag.com/writing-inspiration/ author-interviews/steve-yarbrough/.

"a historic moment for Mississippi."—Page 232, Willie Morris, *Terrains of the Heart and Other Essays on Home* (Oxford, MS: Yoknapatawpha Press, 1981), p. 214–215.

"what it doesn't want to address."—Page 236, Laura M. Holson, "Marking Mississippi's Literary Trail, From William Faulkner to Jesmyn Ward," April 27, 2018. https://www.nytimes.com/2018/04/27/books/ books-mississippi-faulkner-trail.html

BIBLIOGRAPHY

Attaway, William. *Blood on the Forge: A Novel*. Garden City, NY: Doubleday, Doran & Co., Inc, 1941.

Bell, Charles G. *Delta Return*. Bloomington: Indiana University Press, 1956.

Bourgeouis, Louis, editor. *In Our Own Words: Writing from Parchman Prison*. Oxford, MS: VOX Press, 2014.

Brown, Carolyn J. *Song of My Life: A Biography of Margaret Walker*. Jackson: University Press of Mississippi, 2014.

Brown, Larry. *Big Bad Love: Stories*. 1st ed. Chapel Hill, NC: Algonquin Books of Chapel Hill, 1990.

——. *On Fire*. 1st ed. Chapel Hill, NC: Algonquin Books of Chapel Hill, 1993.

Campbell, Will D. *Brother to a Dragonfly*. New York: Continuum, 1992.

Cash, W. J. *The Mind of the South*. New York: Vintage Books, 1960.

Cobb, James C. *The Most Southern Place on Earth: The Mississippi Delta and the Roots of Regional Identity*. New York: Oxford University Press, 1992.

Creekmore, Hubert. *The Chain in the Heart*. New York: Random House, 1953.

——. *The Fingers of the Night*. New York: Appleton-Century Co., Inc., 1946.

——. *Personal Sun: The Early Poems of Hubert Creekmore*. Prairie City, IL: The Village Press, 1940.

——. *The Welcome*. New York: Appleton Century-Crofts, 1948.

Crespino, Joseph. "Mississippi as Metaphor, State, Region, and Nation in Historical Imagination," *Southern Spaces*, October 23, 2006.

Douglas, Ellen. "On the Lake," *The New Yorker*, August 19, 1961, pp. 35–74.

——. *Truth: Four Stories I Am Finally Old Enough to Tell*. Chapel Hill, NC: Algonquin Books of Chapel Hill, 1998.

Dunlap, William. *Short, Mean Fiction*. Oxford, MS: Nautilus Press, 2016.

Dunlap, William, and J. Richard Gruber. *Dunlap*, 1st ed. Jackson: University Press of Mississippi, 2006.

Eubanks, W. Ralph. *Ever Is a Long Time: A Journey Into Mississippi's Dark Past*. New York: Basic Books, 2003.

Faulkner, William. *Absalom, Absalom*. New York: Vintage Books, 1936.

——. *As I Lay Dying: The Corrected Text*. Modern Library ed. New York: Modern Library, 2000.

——. *Go Down, Moses: And Other Stories*. New York: Random House, 1942.

——. *Light in August*, edited by Noel Polk. New York: Vintage Books, 2011.

——. *Sartoris*. New York: Harcourt Brace, 1929.

Ferris, William Reynolds. *Blues From the Delta*. Garden City, NY: Doubleday, 1978.

——. *The South in Color: A Visual Journey*. Chapel Hill: University of North Carolina Press, 2016.

——. *Voices of Mississippi: Artists and Musicians Documented by William Ferris* (3CDs and 1 DVD). Atlanta, GA: Dust to Digital, 2018.

——. *"You Live and Learn. Then You Die and Forget It All": Ray Lum's Tales of Horses, Mules, and Men*. New York: Anchor Books, 1992.

Ford, Richard. *The Sportswriter*. New York: Vintage Books, 1985.

Glissant, Édouard. *Faulkner, Mississippi*. 1st Farrar, Straus and Giroux ed. New York: Farrar, Straus and Giroux, 1999.

Grant, Richard. *Dispatches from Pluto: Lost and Found in the Mississippi Delta*. New York: Simon & Schuster Paperbacks, 2015.

Gussow, Adam. *Beyond the Crossroads: The Devil and the Blues Tradition*. Chapel Hill: University of North Carolina Press, 2017

Hines, Thomas S. *William Faulkner and the Tangible Past: The Architecture of Yoknapatawpha*. Berkeley: University of California Press, 1996.

Hamilton, Mary, Helen Dick Davis, and Ellen Douglas. *Trials of the Earth: The Autobiography of Mary Hamilton.* Jackson: University Press of Mississippi, 1992.

Hannah, Barry. *Airships.* 1ˢᵗ Vintage books ed. New York: Vintage Books, 1985.

———. "The Art of Fiction, No. 184." Issue 172, *The Paris Review,* Winter 2004.

Helferich, Gerard. *High Cotton: Four Seasons in the Mississippi Delta.* New York: Counterpoint, 2007.

Henley, Beth. *Beth Henley: Collected Plays.* 1ˢᵗ ed. Lyme, NH: SK, 2000.

———. *The Jacksonian.* Evanston, IL: Northwestern University Press, 2014.

Hobson, Fred. *Tell About the South: The Southern Rage to Explain.* Baton Rouge: Louisiana State University Press, 1983.

Holland, Endesha Ida Mae. *From the Mississippi Delta: A Memoir.* New York: Simon & Schuster, 1997.

Iles, Greg. *The Bone Tree.* New York: William Morrow, 2015.

———. *Mississippi Blood.* New York: William Morrow, 2017.

———. *Natchez Burning.* New York: Harper Collins, 2014.

Kane, Harnett Thomas. *Natchez on the Mississippi.* New York: William Morrow, 1947.

Key, Harrison Scott. *Congratulations, Who Are You Again? A Memoir.* New York: Harper Perennial, 2018.

Knight, Etheridge. *Born of a Woman: New and Selected Poems.* Boston, MA: Houghton Mifflin, 1980.

———. *The Essential Etheridge Knight.* Pittsburgh, PA: University of Pittsburgh Press, 1986.

Knight, Mary Stanton. "Dear Hubert Creekmore: An Archival Search into the Life of a Queer Mississippi Writer." ProQuest Dissertations Publishing, 2019.

Kornegay, Jamie. *Soil.* New York: Simon and Schuster, 2015.

Laymon, Kiese. *Heavy: An American Memoir.* New York: Scribner, 2018.

———. *How to Slowly Kill Yourself and Others in America: Essays.* Chicago, IL: Bolden, 2013.

———. *Long Division: A Novel.* Chicago, IL: Bolden, 2013.

Mars, Florence, and Lynn Eden. *Witness in Philadelphia.* Baton Rouge: Louisiana State University Press, 1977.

Mason, Gilbert P., and James Patterson Smith. *Beaches, Blood, and Ballots: A Black Doctor's Civil Rights Struggle.* Jackson: University Press of Mississippi, 2000.

Moody, Anne. *Coming of Age in Mississippi.* New York: Dell, 1976.

Morris, Willie. *North Toward Home.* Boston, MA: Houghton Mifflin, 1967.

———. *Terrains of the Heart and Other Essays on Home.* Oxford, MS: Yoknapatapha Press, 1981.

Nezhukumatathil, Aimee. "My South," in *Oceanic.* Port Townsend, WA: Copper Canyon Press, 2018.

Nicholas, Teresa. *Willie: The Life of Willie Morris.* Jackson: University Press of Mississippi, 2016.

Nordan, Lewis. *Boy With Loaded Gun: A Memoir.* New York: Algonquin Books of Chapel Hill, 2000.

———. *Wolf Whistle: A Novel.* New York: Algonquin Books of Chapel Hill, 1993.

O'Connor, Flannery. "Some Aspects of the Grotesque in Southern Fiction," in *Mystery and Manners: Occasional Prose.* New York: Farrar, Strauss and Giroux, 1969.

Percy, Walker. *The Last Gentleman.* New York: Farrar, Straus and Giroux, 1966.

———. *The Moviegoer.* New York: Alfred A. Knopf, 1961.

Percy, William Alexander. *Lanterns on the Levee: Recollections of a Planter's Son.* New York: A.A. Knopf, 1948.

Polk, Noel. *Outside the Southern Myth.* Jackson: University Press of Mississippi, 1997.

Ramsey, Frederic, Jr. *Been here and Gone.* Athens: University of Georgia Press, 2000.

Shearer, Cynthia. *The Celestial Jukebox: A Novel.* Washington, D.C.: Shoemaker & Hoard, 2005.

Silver, James W. *Mississippi: The Closed Society*. New York: Harcourt Brace & World, 1964.

Smith, Katy Simpson. "Why My Students Don't Call Themselves Southern Writers: On Reckoning with a Fraught Literary History," *Lit Hub*, March 13, 2019.

Spencer, Elizabeth. *Landscapes of the Heart: A Memoir*. 1st ed. New York: Random House, 1998.

———. *The Voice at the Back Door*. Baton Rouge: Louisiana State University Press, 1994.

Street, James H. *Look Away: A Dixie Notebook*. New York: The Viking Press, 1936.

———. *Tap Roots*. New York: The Dial Press, 1942.

Taulbert, Clifton L. *When We Were Colored*. New York: Penguin Books, 1995.

Thomas, Angie. *The Hate U Give*. New York: HarperCollins Publishers, 2017

Trethewey, Natasha. *Bellocq's Ophelia: Poems*. Saint Paul, MN: Graywolf Press, 2002.

———. *Beyond Katrina: A Meditation on the Mississippi Gulf Coast*. Athens: University of Georgia Press, 2010.

———. *Domestic Work: Poems*. Saint Paul, MN: Graywolf Press, 2000.

———. *Memorial Drive: A Daughter's Memoir*. New York: Ecco, 2020.

———. *Monument: New and Selected*. Boston, MA: Houghton Mifflin Harcourt, 2018.

———. *Native Guard*. Boston, MA: Houghton Mifflin, 2006.

———. *Thrall: Poems*. Boston, MA: Houghton Mifflin Harcourt, 2012.

Walker, Margaret. *Jubilee*. Boston, MA: Houghton Mifflin, 1966.

Walker, Margaret, and Maryemma Graham. *How I Wrote Jubilee and Other Essays on Life and Literature*. New York: Feminist Press, 1990.

Ward, Jesmyn. *Men We Reaped: A Memoir*. New York: Bloomsbury, 2013.

———. *Salvage the Bones*. New York: Bloomsbury, 2011.

———. *Sing, Unburied, Sing*. New York: Scribner, 2017.

———. *Where the Line Bleeds*. Chicago, IL: Bolden, 2008.

Watkins, Lorie. *A Literary History of Mississippi*. Jackson: University Press of Mississippi, 2017.

Watson, Brad. *Aliens in the Prime of Their Lives: Stories*. New York: W.W. Norton, 2010.

———. *The Heaven of Mercury: A Novel*. New York, W.W. Norton, 2003.

———. *Last Days of the Dog-Men: Stories*. New York: W.W. Norton, 1996.

———. *Miss Jane: A Novel*. New York: W.W. Norton, 2016.

Welty, Eudora. *A Curtain of Green*, introduction by Katherine Anne Porter. Garden City, NY: Doubleday, Doran and Company, Inc, 1941.

———. *Delta Wedding: A Novel*. New York: Harcourt, Brace and Co, 1946.

———. *The Golden Apples*. New York: Harcourt, Brace, 1949.

———. "How I Write," *The Virginia Quarterly Review* 31, no. 2 (1955): 240–251.

———. *Losing Battles*. 1st Vintage Books ed. New York: Vintage Books, 1978.

———. *One Writer's Beginnings*. Cambridge, MA: Harvard University Press, 1984.

———. *On William Faulkner*. Jackson: University Press of Mississippi, 2003.

———. *The Wide Net: And Other Stories*. New York: Harcourt, Brace and Company, 1943.

Wright, Richard. *Black Boy: (American Hunger): A Record of Childhood and Youth*. 1st Perennial Classics ed. New York: Perennial Classics, 1998.

———. *12 Million Black Voices*. New York: Arno Press, 1969.

Yarbrough, Steve. *The Oxygen Man*. Denver, CO: MacMurray and Beck, 1999,

Young, Stark. "Not in Memoriam, but in Defense," in *I'll Take My Stand: The South and the Agrarian Tradition*. Baton Rouge: Louisiana State University Press.

PHOTO CREDITS

Katherine Aberle, pages 240, 252

Courtesy of Kraig Anderson, lighthousefriends.com, page 30

Collection of the Family of Walter Anderson, Copyright the Family of Walter Anderson, page 28

Associated Press Photography, page 85

Courtesy of Belhaven University, page 105

Bloomberg / Getty, page 106 (bottom)

Jim Bourdier / Associated Press, pages 26 (top), 134

Feng Cheng / Shutterstock, page 160

Langdon Clay, page 179

Ed Croom, pages 139, 141, 146, 149, 150, 151, 156, 181

Richard Cummins / Alamy Stock Photo, page 24

Detroit Publishing Company photograph collection. LC-DIG-det-4a24843, page 66 (top); LC-DIG-det-4a13373, page 66 (bottom)

Rory Doyle, pages 16, 186, 189, 229, 237

Abe Draper, pages 130, 132, 135

dszc / iStock, page 26 (bottom)

William Dunlap, courtesy of University of Mississippi Museum, page 137

Pierre Jean Durieu / Dreamstime, page 206 (top)

Edibobb / Wikimedia, page 32

Frank Ezelle, page 111

Photographs by William R. Ferris, William R. Ferris Collection, Southern Folklife Collection, The Wilson Library, University of North Carolina at Chapel Hill: page 75: Left to right (on ground) "Little" Isaiah Brown, Sr., William Ferris, Jr., Allen McGowan, George Martin, Isaiah Brown, Jr., left to right (on truck) Grey Ferris, Ben Guider, Richard Lambert in hay field, Fisher Ferry Road, Warren County, Mississippi, 1963; page 76: Rose Hill Church and Congregation. Left to right, front row: Robert McGowan, Aaron "Dickie"

Thomas (green shirt), Elsa "Pee Wee" McGowan (blue dress), Donald McGowan (gold shirt), Eddie McGowan (yellow shirt), John Henry Wright (gold shirt), Alfred Lee McGowan (white shirt), unidentified woman in green, Brenda Fay Appleton (pink and blue dress), Ida Thomas (blue dress with pink in center), Dessie "Ree" Thomas (green dress with white collar), Diane Wright Smith, Larry "L.S." Huband, Mary "Liz" Martin (pink blouse), Mary Ellen McGowan (under Mary Martin's hands), Patricia "Pat" Price (with bag), Allen "Man" McGowan, Annie "Ann" McGowan (white dress and white hat), Cathy McGowan (green dress), Amanda Gordon (standing in white dress behind Cathy McGowan, unidentified lady with bag, Bertilde Smith (yellow dress and white hat), Dora "Red" Russell (white dress with usher ribbon and white hat, Rosie Wallace (white dress with usher ribbon and white hat), , Rosie McGowan (small girl in front in white dress with usher ribbon and white hat), Allen McGowan (brown suit and gold shirt), Alton McGowan (gold shirt), unidentified young boy in white shirt. Left to right, in doorway: Mary "Monk" Gordon (white hat), Harvey Bass (man in hat), unidentified man without hat, Martha "Tet" Appleton (white dress and hat), Beatrice McGowan (behind Martha Appleton), Betty Ann Thomas (dark blue dress), Lucindy McGriggs (white hat), Mary Lee Appleton (green dress), unidentified man in hat, Steve Washington (gold shirt). Rose Hill Church, Fisher Ferry Road, Warren County, Mississippi, 1975; page 78: S.M. White & Son Crossroads Store, Old Port Gibson Road, Reganton, Mississippi, 1974; page 81: Ray Lum, "The Ketch Pen", Lum Brothers Auction Barn, Vicksburg, Mississippi, 1973; page 244: Parchman Inmates hoeing Cotton, Parchman Penitentiary, Camp B, Lambert, Mississippi, 1974

Gil Ford Photography, Courtesy of the Margaret Walker Foundation, page 109

Michael Ford, pages 176, 180, 183

Christopher Fowler, pages 219, 224

David R. Frazier Photolibrary, Inc. / Alamy Stock Photo, page 91

Craig Hanchey, page 12

Jim Hendrix (www.oxphoto.org), 158

Carol M. Highsmith Archive, Library of Congress, Prints and Photographs Division. LC-DIG-highsm-42504, page 19; LC-DIG-highsm-11865, page 54; LC-DIG-highsm-46994, page 117; LC-DIG-highsm-42197, page 226

Illinois Central Railroad Company 78095_photo.tif / Courtesy of Mississippi Department of Archives and History, page 200

Jackson Daily News / The Clarion-Ledger / PARS International, page 56

jmanaugh3 / Shutterstock, page 165

James Kirkikis / Dreamstime, page 168

morten larsen / Alamy Stock Photo, page 95

Chris Lauer / iStock, page 72

Calvin L. Leake / Dreamstime, page 128

Mike Liu / Shutterstock, page 213

Dennis MacDonald / Alamy Stock Photo, page 70

Jud McCranie / Wikimedia, page 112

Larry McWhorter, page 204

Steve Minor, page 194

©David Rae Morris, page 35, page 171

Mr. Charles C. Mosley, Jr. Courtesy of the Margaret Walker Center, page 106 (top)

Courtesy of the National Park Service, Gulf Islands National Seashore Collection, page 31; Mississippi Gulf Coast National Heritage Area, page 36

Bruce Newman, page 148

Sean Pavone / Shutterstock, page 96

Tom Rankin, page 175

Ann Rayburn Collection of Paper Americana, Archives and Special Collections, University of Mississippi Libraries rayburn_ann_25_07_001, page 51

Steven Reich / iStock, page 6

Steven L. J. Reich / Shutterstock, page 46

Maude Schulyer Clay, page 11

Eric J. Shelton, page 41

Carmen K. Sisson / Cloudybright / Alamy, pages 126, 164, 221

Don Smetzer / Alamy Stock Photo, page 98

Snehitdesign / Dreamstime, page 118

Tabitha Soren, *The Past Does Not Go Quietly*, 2016, page 195; *The Promise of An Obstacle*, 2016, page 198; *Wild and Unwise*, 2016, page 214

Alan Vernon / Getty, page 68

Lindsey M. Walston, page 235

Copyright ©Eudora Welty, LLC; Courtesy Eudora Welty Collection—Mississippi Department of Archives and History, pages 100, 102, 103

Danielle White / Picfair, page 86

Marion Post Wolcott. Farm Security Administration—Office of War Information color slides and transparencies collection. LC-DIG-fsac-1a34351 (Library of Congress), page 190; LC-DIG-fsac-1a34350, page 206 (bottom)

All other photos by the author.

INDEX